POP/ROCK
Question and Answer Book
DAVID DACHS

SBS SCHOLASTIC BOOK SERVICES
New York Toronto London Auckland Sydney

ACKNOWLEDGEMENTS

I would like to thank the following persons and organizations for assistance in acquiring information and photographs: Stu Ginsburg, Capitol Records; Herb Helman, RCA Victor Records; Sol Handwerger, MGM Records; Bob Rolontz, Atlantic Records; Bob Altschuler and Cathy Podlaski, Columbia Records; Ron Oberman, Mercury Records; Marvin Cerf, Marv Greifinger, UA/Liberty Records; Shelley Cooper, Warners-Reprise; Susan Kazak, Buddah Records; Chuck Brown, Solters and Sabinson; Mary Jane Public Relations; Litrov-Levinson; Stan Pakula, ABC-TV Publicity; Dick Williams, Bill Doll Company; Richard Gersh Associates; Hank Rieger, NBC Press; Kassie Gerrick, ABC/Dunhill Records; Tom Trenkle, Gifford-Wallace; Reba Hancock; Harold Leventhal; Josh and Julie Dachs.

Additional credit is given to the following: Michael Mattel, p. 10; Metromedia Records, p. 21; Peter Borsari, pp. 34, 123, 156; UPI, pp. 44, 149; Ken Regan, pp. 55, 70, 72, 79; Curt Gunther, p. 57; Walter Iooss, p. 68; Frank Teti, p. 90; Mike Paladin, p. 162.

1st printing ....April 1971
Printed in the U.S.A.

POP/ROCK
Question and Answer Book

CONTENTS
GROUPS AND STARS

3ob Dylan

THE MUSIC BUSINESS

YOU ASKED FOR IT

- Lynne Thompson of Orlando, Florida, asked Bobby Sherman: "Does singing interfere with girls?" (Answer: "No.")
- Simon and Garfunkel were asked if pop critics in their reviews have to be so "cruel."
- Gary Snyderman of Plymouth Meeting, Pennsylvania, wondered how much pop groups make a year, how much they make at Fillmore East.
- M. Strehlow of Ottawa, Kansas, asked: "What keeps a group together?"

These are just a few of the questions that have been flooding in for the *Pop/Rock Question and Answer Book*. Cartons and cartons of letters from all over the U.S. — small towns in Georgia, New York suburbs, towns in California, remote areas of Texas. Letters came from as far away as Hawaii.

In a way, this is *your* book. It is based on what *you* want to know about the world of pop. Because young people — perhaps you or one of your friends–thought up the questions. In the spring of 1970 an announcement was printed in Scholastic magazines asking readers to send along any questions they had on pop groups, pop songs, singers, the whirling music, and record business.

The mail showed: (1) pop is bigger than bleached blue jeans, and (2) the technicolor trend of papermaking, for letters arrived in all colors — white, raspberry, purple, fuchsia, lemon, and tangerine. Some were short and crisp, like an economically worded telegram. And some ran a dozen pages. Many of the envelopes were decorated with pop-art decals: "Bobby [Sherman] — 4 Ever." Pam Buckingham of Brighton, Michigan, wrote a batch of questions and then on the reverse side of the envelope printed: "Run Mailman Run."

One sticky fact: Not everybody's questions could be used. Many wrote in asking the same questions. So if you wrote in, and your name isn't used, please don't get mad.

Most of the pop stars and pop groups responded. A handful who were on vacation, filling TV schedules, on concert tours, or ill, did not. In those cases, we secured answers from the people close to them — personal managers, record producers, music and record business executives.

There were a variety of questions, and the topics were broad. They ranged from questions of a factual nature about a particular artist or record, to questions which were sharply political — about women's liberation, the role of the pop singer in today's world. Some of the questions weren't questions. One girl invited a pop favorite to her birthday party. Some girls sent in their phone numbers to certain pop stars. Another pop fan in the Southwest wrote inviting a pop idol to visit her city. She would show him around in the deluxe grand manner, and pay all the bills!

And one more thing: Thanks for writing.

— DAVID DACHS

GLEN CAMPBELL

Paul Roberts
Monterey, California
Q. *I heard that your dad forced you to learn and play the guitar. Is that true? Do you approve of this method?*
Glen: Dad never really forced me to do anything, 'cept perhaps helping out with the family chores, which I didn't like too much. But force me to play the guitar — never! There's always been music in my home and if there was any forcing, it was my pleading for a guitar of my own, which Dad bought me from a Sears Roebuck catalogue when I was about five or six years old.

O. Lucyk
Jamaica, New York
Q. *What is your wife's name? Your children's names?*

Glen: My wife's name is Billie Jean. The kiddies are: Kelli, Travis, and our baby, Wesley Kane.

Q. *Are you a good friend of Jim Nabors?*

Glen: Yes, Jim Nabors and I are friends. Mainly I would say professional friends, inasmuch as we have appeared on each other's shows. But if you mean like dropping into each other's homes, or that sort of thing, not really. Socially, at parties and the like, we get together sometimes and chew the fat, and I have a great admiration for Jim's talents.

Philip Balbi
Miami, Florida

Q. *What have been some of the changes in modern country music?*

Glen: I really don't think there have been many changes in country music, not at least the "down home type." Country music, in certain areas, has become a little more sophisticated because people other than country singers are now singing it. Guitars are now sometimes amplified, of course, but the sound is still there, still pure. Country music has gained recognition internationally, and with that comes change. But when you listen to the likes of Merle Haggard and Waylon Jennings, it's still that gutsy, raw, country sound. When you really get down to it, it's not the music that's changed, it's people and their tastes. More and more people have become "aware" of country music — so if there is any real change in it, it's in the fact that it's now as acceptable as any other music in the world.

CREEDENCE CLEARWATER REVIVAL

Mike Phillips
Jackson, Ohio

Q. *I am probably your most avid fan in the state of Ohio, and I have all your albums and am especially fond of* Green River. *It is almost completely worn out! Now for the questions. How can I become a member of the Creedence Clearwater Revival Fan Club?*

Stu Cook: Membership is accomplished by sending $2.00 to P.O. Box 9246, Berkeley, California 94709. You will receive an initial kit that includes group biographies, pictures, button, folder, etc., and our quarterly newsletter. I should mention that the club is run by us, not the record company, and, in general, does not cater to groupies.

Q. *What type of equipment does Doug use? I would like to know since I'm a drummer.*

Doug Clifford: I use Camco equipment. Number one, I'm really satisfied with the sound and tone

qualities. Secondly, I think they are the strongest drums made. This can be really important when you consider the music we play and all the in-person performances. It's really a bummer to break a foot-pedal in the middle of a song.

Q. *I would like to know where the guys in the group hail from?*

Tom Fogerty: We were all born in the San Francisco Bay Area. Stu, John, and I were born in Berkeley, and Doug in Palo Alto. Stu and Doug came to know John in junior high school and I, being John's brother, was soon to follow. We've lived in the Berkeley-El Cerrito area all our lives.

Q. *What do you think of the Beatles break-up?*

John Fogerty: Musically, it's very unfortunate. As a group they were, in my opinion, the greatest, most creative band ever associated with rock music. They were also the biggest act the enter-tainment world has ever seen. As individuals, they have to live their own lives and it's certainly not my place to condemn the break-up. For what they've done to the world of music, I can't thank them. Not enough.

GRASS ROOTS

Ryn Coapu
Bloomington, Indiana
Q. (*To Rob Grill*) *How did you learn to play the bass so well?*

Rob Grill: While attending college I met a guitar player who played lead. He showed me some "licks" and I eventually applied them to the bass. The rest I picked up over the years by playing and learning from friends and some studio musicians. Later I learned to play the guitar and found this to be a great help, as I learned chord structures. [All the notes that go into making a chord.]

FIFTH DIMENSION

Audrey Hull
Dewitt, Virginia
Q. *Where does each individual in your group come from?*
Florence Gordon: All three fellows were born and raised in St. Louis, Missouri, and came to Los Angeles at different times, for different reasons. Marilyn is from Los Angeles (although born in New Jersey). I am from Pennsylvania (though born in New Jersey, also). All members have made Los Angeles their home for the last ten years or more.

Larry Coe
Seguin, Texas
Q. *Do the Fifth Dimension make their own clothes? If so, how?*
Florence: Boyd Clopton has designed and made all the Fifth Dimension's costumes from 1967-69. During the last year we have also had several costumes made and designed by Alan Messinger.

David Fiedler
Forest Hills, New York
Q. *Are concert tours very difficult to make? With regard to travel, food, rest?*
Florence: The Fifth Dimension are proud of their record of having missed only one concert during their career. This was because their plane couldn't land owing to snow. I like the college concerts best of all types of performances, although they are the most tiring, hardest on wardrobe, physical health, and appearance. I try to eat

16

at least one well-balanced meal a day (very few hamburgers), and to rest as much as possible. Now, of course, I'm a mother and when I go on the road I take a nurse along with me and the baby. The baby's first trip was to Japan, at the age of one month.

Marilyn McCoo: Yes, concert tours are extremely difficult, although they are the most rewarding. College students are very open-minded to all kinds of music, and they are very responsive and polite. One of the biggest problems facing the group on one-nighters is that we can never predict difficulties that arise with airlines or buses that we charter in relation to the weather conditions or road conditions. Once the group had a flat tire in a chartered bus on the road at 4:00 A.M. On another occasion, again on a chartered bus, the highway was slick because of ice, and the bus almost slid into a gully. It's a wonder we're still around!

TOMMY JAMES

Reinhard Quast
Cedar Lake, Michigan
Q. *Why haven't I seen any albums of yours here in Cedar Lake, Michigan?*
Tommy: I suggest you write to Roulette Records, 17 West 60th Street, New York, N.Y., for information on where you might find some of my albums.
Q. *Which is your own favorite record?*
Tommy: "Helpless" by Crosby, Stills, and Nash. (Atlantic Records)

Melba Alford
Morrison, Tennessee
Q. *How old are you and are you married?*
Tommy: I am 23 years old and am married. My wife's name is Ronnie and I live in Manhattan.

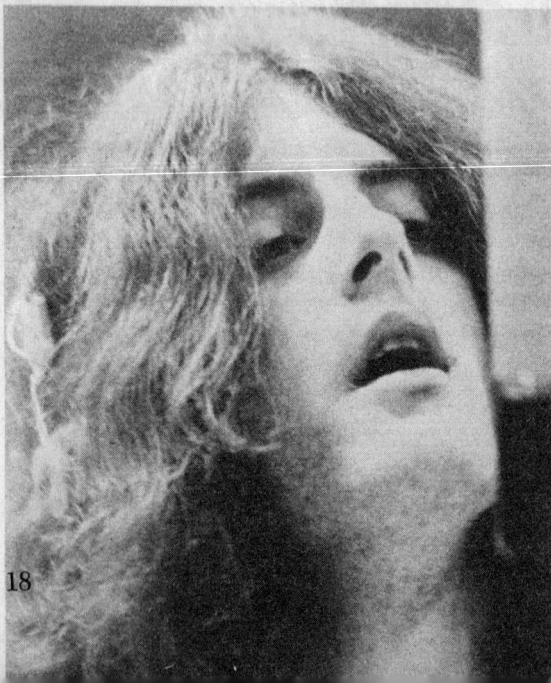

BOBBY SHERMAN

Laura Lansen
Little Suomico, Wisconsin
Q. *What do you think of all the drugs the kids are taking nowadays? Do you think it's wise or not?*
Bobby: I think that taking drugs is the worst thing anybody can do to their body and their mind.

Margaret Cressel
Alexandria, Virginia
Q. *I would like to know if you received a song written by a fan if you would use it if you liked it?*
Bobby: Yes I would — but only if the song came from a publisher. There are just too many legal problems involved with using a song that comes through the mail.

Terry Rickey
Scottsburg, Indiana
Q. *We're starting a fan club in our school called "Our Dream Bobby Sherman." What town are you from and what school did you attend?*
Bobby: I was born in Santa Monica, California, and I attended Gault Elementary and Birmingham High School in Van Nuys.

Vickie Saltars
Tipton, Iowa
Q. *What is your favorite color?*
Bobby: Blue.

G. Slotnick
Wantagh, New York
Q. *How many records have you put out, and will you continue to be on* Here Come the Brides?
Bobby: Although it seems like a lot more, because of the fact that I have been fortunate enough to get a great deal of air play, I've only recorded five singles and two albums. As for my continuing with *Here Come the Brides*, it's been cancelled, so I guess I won't.

Ruth-Ann Sardo
Harrington Park, New Jersey
Q. *What influences the selection of a flip side for your single records, and why was the flip side selection of "Easy Come, Easy Go" changed from "Sounds Along the Way" to "July Seventeen"?*
Bobby: The only thing that influences the selection of a flip side on my singles is what we consider the second best song. In regard to the switch from "Sounds" to "July Seventeen" simply

this — the latter wasn't ready soon enough, so a few copies went with "Sounds," and as soon as the editing was ready, we completed the pressing with that, as it was our first choice.

Wilma Brown
Helena, Montana
Q. *Who makes your records?*
Bobby: Metromedia manufactures and releases my records. If you're talking about the sessions themselves: On the date for "Julie, Do You Love Me?" Jackie Miles was the producer and Al Capps, the arranger.

Ellen and Ann Rubin
Huntington, New York
Q. *What is your favorite town, city, or state?*
Bobby: My pet cities are Los Angeles and New York.

Karen Moreth
Bradford, Pennsylvania
Q. *Are you fond of animals? If so, what kind?*
Bobby: I have a dog, Dopey, and I love him.

Brenda Woodward
Gainesville, Florida
Q. *What is your favorite town, city, or state?*
Bobby: My pet cities are Los Angeles and New and The Doors.

Kim Elliott
Springfield, Massachusetts
Q. *What other TV programs have you been on?*
Bobby: I was on *Shindig*, a rock musical variety program, for about two years. I have had guest

starring roles in *Honey West, The Monkees,* and *The F.B.I.* Of course, my biggest role so far has been as Jeremy Bolt, the youngest of three brothers who own a logging camp in Seattle at the turn of the century in *Here Come the Brides.*

Jo Ann and Sandy Cardwell
West Hamlin, West Virginia
Q. *Have you ever had a gold record?*
Bobby: I've been pretty lucky. In just a very brief time, I've managed to collect three gold singles ("Hey, Little Woman," "La, La, La," and "Easy Come, Easy Go") and two gold albums.

Ann Marie Stalica
Schenectady, New York
Q. *Are you going to have your own TV show?*
Bobby: I hope so. I'm working on a few things now.
Q. *Are you going to appear in any movies?*
Bobby: Roles are being offered me.
Q. *Are you going to be making any concert tours in 1971?*
Bobby: I'll be making personal appearances in 1971.

Diane Dupont
Taunton, Massachusetts
Q. *Is it true that Bobby Sherman started his career at a party?*
A. While still in high school, where he studied engineering and played football, Bobby's extra-curricular activities included singing at parties. Among those who heard him at a Hollywood affair one evening were Natalie Wood, Sal Mineo,

Jane Fonda, and Roddy McDowall. The foursome was so impressed with Bobby's talents, they took him under their collective wing to sponsor his career. A result of his celebrated mentors' faith in their young protégé was his first recording contract.

Another, even more fortuitous break followed when Bobby auditioned for a new television show, *Shindig*. Winning out over more than 500 other young aspirants, he was chosen to star on the show, which was on the air almost two years.

Sherman immediately became an idol of his contemporaries over the nation. For eight consecutive months, his fan mail topped that of any other performer on the entire ABC network. And when the *Shindig* cast threw a surprise oncamera birthday party for him, the show was inundated with more than 10,000 birthday cakes from adoring fans!

He plays 11 instruments: drums, trumpet, guitar, bass, french horn, trombone, baritone (small) tuba, piano, organ, sitar, and harmonica. Because he likes to experiment with new recording techniques, he designed and constructed his own recording studio, at his parents' home in San Fernando Valley.

Kay Woodruff
San Leandro, California

Q. *What does Bobby think about Love and Peace?*

A. Apparently he's very much for both. He wears love beads, and a peace ring, and at personal appearances he flashes the two-fingered peace sign.

Teresa Foisy
Springfield, Massachusetts

Q. *I hear that Bobby Sherman is 24. Is it true?*
A. He's 26. He was born July 22, 1944.

Q. *Does Bobby have many fans?*
A. Don't ask! He's one of the hottest pop stars around these days. There is a virtual Bobby Sherman industry. You can buy mail order — Bobby Sherman love beads, Bobby Sherman peace rings, Bobby Sherman love necklaces, Bobby Sherman's Concert Photo Album, Bobby Sherman's Official Concert Poster. The fan magazines are full of Bobby Shermania. Sample magazine stories: "You Can Go Back Stage with Bobby," "Bobby Sherman on TV," "Sing Along with Bobby Sherman," "Bobby's Love List." You can even enter a contest and "Win the Shirt Off Bobby Sherman's Back."

HOW TO START A
POP GROUP

Deborah Jacobs
Bristol, Pennsylvania

Q. *I was just wondering if you could help me out. I'm planning to get a group together.*

According to **Richard Gersh**, one of the top pop publicists, whose accounts include the Fifth Dimension and The Who, here are five tips:

1. The first thing a new group has to do is make a tape. The tape should be the very best you can make, whether it's in a garage, or a studio. Edit it, re-edit it. Go over it again and again until you're sure it's the best the group can do.

2. In making the tape, make sure that the tape contains some original material. Maybe two familiar tunes and two originals. The record company wants to hear what a new group can do with new material.

3. Know what's happening. Be show-wise. Obtain copies of the music business tradepapers: *(Cash Box, Variety, Record World, Billboard).* Learn which companies are the most active. See who's on the charts. Send your tape to the most active companies — those in the Top Ten. Don't send it to some sleepy firm. If you have any doubts about where to send the tape, check with your local radio station or disc jockey.

4. Have the original material copyrighted. Nobody is looking for lawsuits, and some people are reluctant to look at material unless it's copyrighted. For this reason, contact a local lawyer regarding legal protection.

5. Let's say the record company has responded. They're interested. Well, make sure you have legal representation to speak for you. Do not sign any long-term contracts with personal managers or booking offices. Try to hold off for as long as possible before committing yourself. Lots of groups have broken up because they've gotten themselves involved with managers or booking offices they hate. Every day you do not sign with a personal manager you're better off. You have another day to make a decision you can live with. With the record company you don't have to be so careful. They're not interested in taking advantage. They are out for your best interests.

BLACK-OWNED RECORD COMPANIES

Michael Williams
St. Albans, New York

Q. *Have there been any black-owned record companies before Motown?*

A. Blacks, of course, have made great contributions to performing, composing, lyric-writing, record-producing. However, there have been few wholly owned black record companies. The first all-black disc company was Black Swan Records, which was active in the '30's. The late W. C. Handy, composer of "St. Louis Blues," had a half-interest. In modern times, of course, the big, black-owned record company is Motown and its subsidiary labels Tamla and Gordy, owned by Berry Gordy, Jr. An ex-worker on the Detroit assembly line, and a former songwriter, he started it all with a $700 loan.

JOE SOUTH

Penelope Coronel
Waianae, Hawaii

Q. *When performing, what kind of feeling do you get?*

Joe: I love it. I love the feel of a live audience, the response it gives you. A real warm feeling. It's funny really, I started performing when I was real young — and I guess what they say about kids having no fear is surely real, because I never did. Then I gave up actual performing for a while and concentrated on writing for, and producing, other artists. I also did some session back-up work, but there came a point when I realized that that wasn't making it for me, and so I started out in the world of performing again. The second time around I was a little nervous to begin with, but

I soon got back into the swing of it, and then did I ever realize what I'd been missing!

Alden Solovy
Chicago, Illinois
Q. *How do you feel when you're recording?*
Joe: Recording is fun, and I guess I get almost the same kind of satisfaction from that as I do from performing. I like being on both sides of the fence — as a performer and as a producer. I have my own studios in Atlanta, and most days, when I'm not off doing a gig somewhere, I'll be puttering around the studios playing with this sound or that sound, or adding a melody to some tune I've written. I guess I'm just totally involved in my music — or at least that's my excuse!

Andrea Freund
White Plains, New York
Q. *After years of trying to make it big with a record, how does it feel to have lots of hits and gold records?*
Joe: It feels just great. I guess every artist is striving for recognition and acceptance; that's what a hit record means — acceptance. And I'm lucky in that I get it different ways. For instance, my song "Games People Play" was a hit for me and a country hit for Freddy Weller. Then Della Reese did it on her TV show and invited me to join her, so she sang it her way — real slow and bluesy — and I sang it mine, and was that ever a gas!

Gary Snyderman
Plymouth Meeting, Pennsylvania
Q. *How long does it take you to cut an album?*

Joe: Oh, man, does that ever depend. Sometimes I'll just stay in the studios till it's done — day and night, if necessary — but that's just me. I don't expect anyone else to try it, it can be mighty tiring. But I guess what I'm trying to say is I don't have any set schedule for myself and I've probably never counted in realms of hours or days or whatever. I'll play with my tunes and get them how I like them. Then the musicians will come in and join me and we'll gig for a while, and then get something down on tapes — so it's a real natural thing for us.

EASY RIDER[?]

Beverlea Cale
Wilmington, Delaware
Q. *For Easy Rider: How did you get started?*
A: So far as our research goes, there is no Easy Rider group. You must be referring to the film. In it the score was performed by many pop groups and singers, including The Byrds. All the music can be heard on the soundtrack LP *Easy Rider* (Dunhill). The film, of course, starred Peter Fonda.

RAY STEVENS

Roberta Class
Watertown, Connecticut
Q. *Did you write any of your songs?*

Ray: Almost everything. Wrote all the big hits I've had, "Gitarzan," "Ahab the Arab," "Mr. Businessman," "Along Came Jones," "Isn't It Lonely Together."
Q. *Who wrote "Everything Is Beautiful"?*
Ray: I did.

Richard Dachs
Brooklyn, New York
Q. *How did you get started?*
Ray: My parents thought I had a musical talent and started me on piano lessons at five. I continued to study classical piano for 16 years and gradually moved away from classical. I felt it wasn't really my area. I needed more freedom.

FINDING RECORDS

Reinhard Quast
Cedar Lake, Michigan

Q. *Are there any special places where you can buy records that are no longer in the normal record shops?*

A. Local record shops, department stores, dime stores rarely stock records in depth. Most concentrate on the current best sellers. One of the biggest sources for hard-to-get records is Sam Goody's, 235 W. 49th Street, New York, N.Y. Send them a list of records you are hunting for. If they have them they will inform you and tell you how much they cost. Another excellent source that stocks thousands of records most record shops don't have is King Karol. Write them at P.O. Box 629, Times Square Station, New York, N.Y. 10036. Another good source for discs that aren't easily available is The House of Oldies, 267 Bleecker Street, New York, N.Y. 10014. It specializes in old pop singles and LP hits — the golden oldies. A good collection of oldies from 1955 to 1969, with the original artists, is also available at the Blue Note Shop, 156 Central Avenue, Albany, New York 12206. It concentrates wholly on 45 rpm singles.

TOM JONES

O. Lucyk
Jamaica, New York
Q. *How old are you? How tall?*
Tom: 30. 6 feet.
Q. *What group do you like best?*
Tom: All groups.
Q. *Who is your favorite actor?*
Tom: Paul Newman.
Q. *What is your wife's name?*
Tom: Linda.

Cathy Ardolino
Brooklyn, New York
Q. *Do you spend much time with your family or is most of it devoted to your work?*
Tom: As much as possible with my family.

Paula Ann Durniak
Auburn, New York
Q. *Every thursday night I watch* This Is Tom Jones. *At the end of the show you say something in Welsh and then say "No star." Could you please tell me what this means?*
Tom: May you all be well and happy — good night.
Q. *Also, those girls who sit in the audience, are they paid to scream and kiss you? Are they from the studio or are they just an ordinary audience?*
Tom: Ordinary audience.
Q. *Have there been any men in the audience?*
Tom: From time to time, if they care to drop in.

UNDERGROUND RADIO

Mathew Friedman
Los Angeles, California

Q. *What is underground radio?*

Sol Handwerger, MGM Records Publicity Director: Underground radio stations are controversial stations that will play recordings that are sometimes (a) suggestive, supersexy, (b) have to do with drugs, (c) contain strong political statements. They consist of some college and some commercial stations. They do it primarily to woo the young audiences, to give them a competitive edge. Then they approach big advertisers and say they reach the youth market. College audiences lean to underground radio.

Paul Brown, record promotion specialist: Underground stations are mostly FM stations. To find another type of music to play they settled on the off-beat music. They helped to make stars of Grand Funk Railroad; Blood, Sweat and Tears; and many others. College radio is growing, too, and I expect in the next five years every college in the United States will have its own station. Today, there are over 600 college radio stations. Every record company has seen the value of college radio. They are hiring promotion people just to promote records on the college stations. Artists made popular by college radio are Janis Ian, Joe Cocker, Melanie, and Spooky Tooth, just to mention a few. These stations are run by students and they do a great job.

MARK LINDSAY

Kathy Lons
Cleveland, Ohio
Q. *Why did you cut off your pony tail?*
Mark: I had a beard which I shaved off for the Grammy's and since ponytails are so common these days I cut it off too.

Andrea Freund
White Plains, New York
Q. *After years of trying to make it big with a record, how does it feel to have lots of hits and gold records?*
Mark: It really feels good. It makes you want to go on and make more gold records.

Gary Snyderman
Plymouth Meeting, Pennsylvania
Q. *How long does it take to cut an album?*
Mark: Anywhere from one week to two months, depending on how much time we have to work with.

THE JACKSON 5

Pat Ann Jones
Jacksonville, Florida

Q. *What are the names and ages of the Jackson 5?*

A. Here's the rundown on the Jackson 5:

Michael: He's ten. Born August 29, 1960. Lead singer, his healthy, cleancut looks have made him a top favorite. He's a self-taught dancer, moves easily on his feet. According to his family, he's got an extra helping of "soul." Some say that the way he moves about, sings, clowns around puts him into the tradition of singer-dancer Sammy Davis, Jr. Smallish, he could be lost in a wingchair. Likes rope-climbing, has pet mice.

Marlon is about a year older than Michael. Born March 12, 1959. He goes to junior high school. He helps work out some of the basic steps and floor patterns the Jackson 5 use on stage.

Jermaine: He's 15. Born December 11, 1955. He plays the bass. They say he has the best musical ear. Now attending junior high school, he was lead singer till Michael took over.

Toriano (Tito): 17 years old. Born August 15, 1953. He's the guitar player of the group. Got a feeling for tools and working with his hands. Most recently he made a go-cart from an old lawn mower and a few other scrap parts.

Jackie: He's the oldest, 18. Born May 4, 1952. His real name is Sigmund, but the Jackson family call him "Jackie." Highly sports-minded. He has won many plaques and trophies in baseball and basketball. He plays when not in class, in rehearsal, or on stage.

They make up the Jackson 5, but the family pop group may soon become the Jackson 6. Waiting in the wings and ready to go on is seven-year-old Randy. He sings, and shakes a mean bongo.

Q. *I have never really seen a picture of them.*
A. Here they are.

Carolyn Jackson
Springfield, Massachusetts
Q. *Who gave them the idea to start the group?*
A. The story goes somewhat like this: The father worked as a crane operator in Gary, Indiana. But in his spare time, Joe Jackson dreamed of becoming a big-time musician. Away from the quivering controls of the steel lift, he worked out chords on the guitar, wrote songs. His wife, Katherine, also had a feeling for music. She sang country and western tunes, with a touch of soul. When the Jackson children started growing up, they took to mama's and papa's homemade music.

Look magazine has described the early days of the Jackson 5 before they got to be "the hottest new group in the record world." It reported: "When his sons began to show a musical flair — Michael was only four at the time — Jackson began entering them in amateur talent contests, first in Gary, then around the state. Trundling about the East in a Volkswagen bus, the group branched out into weekend gigs [jobs] at colleges or in black theatres. In 1969 Gary's black mayor, Richard Hatcher, introduced them to Diana Ross, star of the Supremes [now on her own]. She helped them cop a Motown contract."

Q. *Does the Jackson 5 have any other brothers or sisters?*

A. Yes, there's young Randy, referred to earlier. And there are three Jackson girls, Maureen, 20, Letoya, 14, and Janet, 4.

Rosalind Bates
Ooltewah, Tennessee
Q. *Where do the Jackson 5 live now?*
A. Since they have become top juke box favorites with their brand of simple love songs, the Jackson 5 have moved from Gary, Indiana, to Beverly Hills, California. There, they have a big private home, with a swimming pool and a practice room where they can play and sing undisturbed. Mindful of show business corruption, the Jackson parents are trying hard to keep the schoolboys from being swell-headed. Guiding them in the transition from the working class steel-town atmosphere of Gary to the lush surroundings of Beverly Hills is Berry Gordy, Jr. He is the enormously successful head of Motown Records. An ex-Detroit auto worker, he is owner of the first major black-controlled record company in the United States. Gordy is very high on the Jackson 5. He says: "The Jackson 5 are five lovable boys, well brought up. And Michael Jackson has that rare star quality everyone looks for. The minute I saw Michael and the group I knew they had the potential."

The boys have a detailed daily program — studies, rehearsals, learning new songs, checking out dance steps with Motown assistance, and regular school homework. They are all supposed to be in bed by 10 P.M. They are the darlings of the fan magazines. They quote young Michael on his philosophy about "going steady." Photographs of them are always played up. Sample: "Sweethearts of the Month in color — The Jackson 5."

Q. *How many records have the Jackson 5 made?*
A. At this writing the Jackson 5 have produced two big best-selling singles, "I Want You Back," and "A B C." "I Want You Back" proved to be an instant smash. It hit the number one spot on all the recognized top-forty charts in both the United States and Great Britain and sold upward of 3,000,000 copies. The recording of "A B C" climbed to gold record status in less than two weeks. They also have two albums out: *Diana Ross Presents the Jackson 5* and *A B C*. More Jackson recordings are on their way.

Interestingly enough, the rock newspaper, *Rolling Stone,* which can be pretty rough in their disc reviews, didn't throw any stones at Jackson 5's LP, *A B C*. In fact, they liked it very much. "*A B C* is an album wholly in the spirit of those great Jackson 5 singles, two of which, the title cut and the incredible 'The Love You Save,' are included. Catchy melodies, explosive rhythm backgrounds, and energetic vocals are the rule here, especially on the first side, which is as strong as anyone could want."

GROUP TOGETHERNESS

M. Strehlow
Ottawa, Kansas
Q. *What keeps a group together?*
Randy Cain, The Delfonics: Having hit records and touring all over the country has been quite an experience. We've all learned more about ourselves and how to work together for a common goal. We've learned to think as a group instead of just three individuals.

Alden Solovy
Chicago, Illinois
Q. *Why do groups break up?*
A. One important record executive, who refused to be named, had this to say: "When they're starting out, they're all friends. They work their hearts out. They rehearse long hours. They starve. They're trying to preach a message through the songs. They're not interested in money. Then they get a hit record. Soon they can't stand each other. They say one is better than another. And the group breaks up. Not one big group has stayed together, including the Beatles. It's a farce. They claim they're all ethical people, in it for moral reasons, to spread the message, but all they are interested in is the almighty buck."

ENGELBERT HUMPERDINCK

Beverlea Cale
Wilmington, Delaware

Q. *How did you get started?*

Engelbert: I was one of ten children. As a young man I worked in a glove factory. I had a great urge to sing. For about ten years I went on singing in workingmen's pubs in England for a bare minimum. Nothing much happened to me professionally those years, and I also had some health problems including a touch of TB. Then Gordon Mills, who's also the manager of Tom Jones, discovered me. He renamed me Engelbert Humperdinck. It was a long, hard struggle. At one time my family was assisted by the British equivalent of welfare.

44

Joan Desccomny
Philadelphia, Pennsylvania

Q. *What is your real name?*

Engelbert: Arnold George Dorsey.

Q. *Is it true that you and Tom Jones are good friends?*

Engelbert: Yes.

Q. *What kind of car do you have?*

Engelbert: I have several cars. A Phantom G. Rolls; Silver Shadow Rolls; Mercedes Benz.

Q. *Do you have false sideburns?*

Engelbert: My hair and sideburns are real.

Q. *Where do you live?*

Engelbert: Weybridge, Surrey.

Q. *What was your first hit record?*

Engelbert: "Release Me."

Q. *What do you think about America and American fans? How do they differ from English fans?*

Engelbert: Love America — love American and English fans.

TV MONEY

Andrea Goldman
Concord, California

Q. *How much do pop groups and pop stars make on television?*

A. Rick Bernstein, Creative Management Associates: On the 90-minute talk shows (Johnny Carson, Dick Cavett, Merv Griffin) the union minimum is $265 plus 10 per cent agency fees. The buyer pays the 10 per cent agency commission. A five-member pop group will get $795. An eight-member pop group will receive $1192. After eight it's $132 per person. If a pop star or group is woven into a situation comedy program on television the fees are shaped by the Screen Actors Guild. The union minimum is $120 a day per actor. However, for a name pop star or pop group the figure is negotiable — how much they can get from the TV producers. The guest star fees that a pop star or pop group gets on an Ed Sullivan or Glen Campbell variety show vary. It goes from $1500 for a brand new act or personality, to the top-of-the-show figure, which is $7500. A Fifth Dimension or Tony Bennett will receive $7500. In rare cases, such as an appearance by The Beatles, the figure can go to $10,000.

SONNY JAMES

Deborah Gokey
Newport, New York
Q. *Are you married?*
Sonny: Yes.
Q. *Is the drummer with your orchestra some relation of yours?*
Sonny: No.

Jennifer Heftler
Valley Stream, New York
Q. *How can I become a singer?*
Sonny: It is very hard to "become a singer." If you are blessed with the God-given ability to sing, it is a simple matter of practice of the type of singing that you enjoy. That's the best way to increase your ability. It helps, of course, to take lessons and learn the technical details of singing in school or from private teachers. Then, if you are lucky and all goes well, possibly you will become a professional favorite.

STEPPENWOLF

Greg Romano
Watertown, Connecticut
Q. *What is your favorite song?*

John Kay: The one I am listening to at the moment.

Jerry Edmonton: The Rolling Stones' "Let It Bleed."

George Biondo: I feel I cannot answer the question as I like too many things.

Goldy McJahn: Jimmy McGriff's "I've Got a Woman."

Q. *What are your real names?*

Goldy McJahn: John Raymond Goadsby

Larry Clifton Byron: Larry Clifton Byron

John Kay: Joachim Fritz Krauledat

George Biondo: George Michael Biondo

Jerry Edmonton: Gerald Michael McCrohan

BACH TO ROCK

Melanie Morris
New York, New York

Q. *Does a pop group that plays classical music in addition to rock stimulate an interest in classical music among rock fans?*

New York Rock Ensemble: Apparently the group does stimulate an interest in classical music among rock fans (or among young college audiences in general). For example, a Pennsylvania college has asked us to come back with a string section and a more classically oriented program. One Colorado college has asked us to send our own orchestrations and rehearse their student orchestra for participation in a program there. When the Boston Symphony Orchestra booked us to play a concert which was being video taped, a portion of the audience seemed to develop a new interest in rock as a musical experience. The video tape was dynamite and has been aired twice on educational TV networks. This kind of activity is being limited now, since after years of touring the group is evolving into a rock group and beginning to break out a bit.

THE COWSILLS

Nancy Lewis
Watervliet, New York
Q. *I would like to know the birthdays of each member of the family.*
A. Bob: August 6, 1949
Paul: November 11, 1952
Barry: September 14, 1954
John: March 2, 1956
Susan: May 21, 1959

DONNY OSMOND

Sheila Reed
Knoxville, Tennessee

Q. *How did you start singing?*

Donny: My brothers led the way. They sang as a quartet for quite awhile before I got interested. My first public appearance was in Chicago when I was five years old, as I remember. We all got started, really, by entertaining our family at home. We've always had Family Night on Friday night (with dinner by candlelight). After our

meal, we'd take turns putting on a program.

Q. *What kind of music do you like?*

Donny: I like R&B [rhythm and blues] and rock.

Q. *Where do you live?*

Donny: Our real home is in Utah. We have one in the San Fernando Valley in California, too. But we travel about nine months a year. So our home is wherever we check in for the night — or the week — or the month. We travel together as a family (nine of us). My two older brothers are attending college in Utah. One of them is married now, so they don't go with us. They often attend our performances when we are in Las Vegas, though.

Clare Frank
Wawaka, Indiana

Q. *Do you have any brothers and sisters not in the group?*

Donny: Virl and Tom used to be a tap dance team. They both have a hearing loss, so weren't able to sing with us. They're excellent dancers though, but gave up show business to fill a two-year mission for our church. (We're Mormons.) We have one sister, Marie, age ten [she'll be 11 in October]. She sings and dances with us occasionally. She hasn't been too interested in the entertainment field, but she did some pretty good performances in Japan — even recorded a little there — so we may see more of her in the future.

Q. *Who taught you to play your instrument?*

Donny: Mother taught me how to play the saxophone and Alan taught me how to play the organ and to understand all the chords.

Q. *How many instruments do you play? And which are they?*

Donny: I play the saxophone, piano, and organ.

Q. *How did you meet Andy Williams?*

Donny: Andy's father saw the quartet (Alan, Wayne, Merrill, and Jay) on television from Disneyland one night. They reminded him of the Williams Brothers when they got started, and he thought it would be a novelty to have them on the show, Andy's show. He called us in Utah and asked us to come and audition.

Teresa Chambers
Weaverville, North Carolina

Q. *I read in one of the editions of* Fave *magazine that Donny Osmond is 13 and in* Tiger Beat *it said he was 11. Will you please tell me which is right?*

A. Here are the vital statistics on Donny:

    Age: 13
    Birthday: December 9, 1957
    Hair: Light brown
    Eyes: Brown

They say that Donny causes young girls to get weak in the knees. He's known as the "lady killer." He was seen as an actor in the short-lived TV series, *The Travels of Jamie McPheeters*. Along with his brothers, Donny has a lot of fans abroad, particularly in Japan. Originally the Osmond Brothers were under contract to Barnaby Records, a company started by Andy Williams. Now they record for MGM. Their first two releases in the summer of 1970 were "Movin' Along," and "Open Your Heart."

BUCK OWENS

Louise Glover
Denton, North Carolina

Q. *How old are you?*

Buck: I am 40 years old. My birthday is August 12.

Q. *Are you self-taught?*

Buck: I am a self-taught musician. When I was 13 years old, my mother gave me a mandolin which I learned to play by myself; and in the next few years I also learned to master the guitar.

Q. *How did you get started?*

Buck: My first professional job was in Mesa, Arizona, when I had my own nightly radio show. I was working with a group called the Skillet Lickers at that time, but broke away from them when I moved to Bakersfield in 1951. My first jobs here in Bakersfield were at country clubs in the area, where I played lead guitar. One night the singer was ill and the owner of the club asked me to take his place. After that he decided that I would be the lead singer from then on. My first records were on Starday labels; and after some minor success with them, I was signed by Ken Nelson to a Capitol Records' contract. After my first hit single, things became much easier for me; and since then, every single I have released has reached the No. 1 spot on the national charts.

Q. *Which kind of music do you listen to?*

Buck: I like all types of music but, of course, my favorite is country music. To me country music is the music of the American people and should be called American music. My favorite songs include those of Merle Haggard and Jimmy Webb. I also think that many of the songs brought out by Creedence Clearwater are very adaptable to the country music audiences. Of the many songs that I have written myself, my favorite has always been "Together Again."

THE RASCALS

Robert Itkin
West Orange, New Jersey

Q. *Who's considered the best rock drummer?*
Eddie Brigati, The Rascals: Dino Danelli.
Q. *Who's considered the best lead guitarist?*
Eddie: Eric Clapton.
Q. *The best bass guitarist?*
Eddie: Paul McCartney.
Q. *The best organist?*
Eddie: Jimmy Smith.
Q. *The best vocalist in terms of voice quality?*
Eddie: Dionne Warwick and Eddie Brigati (potentially).

JOSE FELICIANO

Michael Williams
St. Albans, New York

Q. *When did you know you were going to make it?*

Jose: Well, I'll be honest with you. I didn't know I was going to make it. I mean, an artist never knows whether he's going to make it or not. One — you can believe that but you don't know whether it's going to come true or not. And when it happened to me, it just happened really fast — and it just spun me around.

MERLE HAGGARD

Gary Snyderman
Plymouth Meeting, Pennsylvania
Q. *How long does it take to cut a record?*
Merle: The length of time depends on each individual album. You never really can tell exactly.
It may take you ten takes to get just one number,
or you may do it in one take. Normally, though,
when I'm planning on cutting an album, we'll be
in the studio a total of, I guess, 12 hours or so for
actual recording, then possibly another couple of
hours overdubbing if necessary, or sweetening,
which means perhaps adding strings or something.

Alden Solovy
Chicago, Illinois
Q. *How do you feel when you're recording?*
Merle: When I record — that's just the greatest.
I feel more comfortable recording than anything
else, I think. When I go into a studio with my

group, The Strangers, and we can kick around ten or twelve tunes and get them on tape as we want to hear them, there's no happier man around. My producer at Capitol, Ken Nelson, has been producing my records for a long time. We know and understand each other. He knows when to let me have my head, to let me stop a song in the middle and change the instrumentation line-up, to go into a different key if I think the overall sound will be better — it's just a gas to record and I love every minute of it. Also, when I'm recording down in Hollywood, it's usually after a tour, and some of our tours are real long and tiring. At the end of the day, I can just relax and chew the fat with the guys, and we don't have to go dashing off to the next town, so I guess you could say that recording is a kind of rest therapy for me.

Penelope Coronel
Waianae, Hawaii
Q. *When performing, what kind of feeling do you get?*
Merle: One word can sum up the answer to that question, at least when I first walk out on stage — nervous! When I'm in front of an audience, even though I love to sing and perform, I still get nervous. The reason for that, I guess, is that I am really not yet completely satisfied with myself as a performer. I love to sing, write songs, and record, but when I'm performing I always get the feeling that I can do better and must do better. It's easier for me now than it used to be, and I guess when you love something enough, faith in it will overcome everything.

BOB DYLAN

David Seidman
Tacoma Park, Maryland

Q. *What is Bob Dylan's stand on Viet Nam, pollution, gun control, etc.?*

A. There's a nylon curtain around Bob Dylan. You know he's around, but you can't reach him. Occasionally people see him at an off-Broadway show. He now lives in Greenwich Village in New York City, but you can't reach him too easily to ask questions. Pop music writers who approach Columbia Records regarding interviews with Dylan are told "Forget it!" One must assume, based on the past, that he is, of course, against pollution and war. He has never made his position publicly clear on the Viet Nam war nor has he appeared at recent anti-Viet Nam war rallies with fellow pop artists. His stand on legislation regarding gun control is also unknown. He seems determined to keep away from politics. Bob Dylan is 30 years old (born May 24, 1941). He is the father of four children, including Maria and Jesse. He continues to write songs, put out records. He draws, too, and you can see an example of his work on the record jacket of *Self-Portrait*.

Vicki Thayer
Toms River, New Jersey

Q. *When did Bob Dylan have his first hit?*
A. Actually Bob Dylan first won public attention as a song writer rather than as a recording artist. In 1963, wiry Bob Dylan, then 22 years old, walked into Gerde's, a folk night club in Greenwich Village, New York City, with a new song he had just written, "Blowin' in the Wind." It was recorded by Peter, Paul, and Mary and rose to become a No. 1 hit. As a recording artist Dylan did pretty well for the first few years, but it wasn't until 1967 that he really exploded. In August of that year, he had three LP's win Gold Records. They were: *Blonde on Blonde, Highway 61, Bringing It All Back Home.* He continued his streak of hits with *Bob Dylan's Greatest Hits,* and *John Wesley Harding* (1968), *Nashville Skyline* (1969), *Self-Portrait* (1970), and *New Morning* (1970).

BLUES IMAGE

Vicki Thayer
Toms River, New Jersey

Q. *Is "Ride, Captain, Ride" by the Blues Image the story of Noah's Ark and his trip with the animals?*

A. Noah was a God-fearing figure in Genesis picked by God to save some people and animals during a mammoth flood. To preserve them, he built a 450-foot ship called the Ark. Noah warned the people about the flood, that it was coming. But they didn't believe him. However his craft did ride out the storm which lasted 40 days and 40 nights. The song recorded by the Blues Image (Atco) tells the story of 73 men who sail in a mystery ship to another shore from San Francisco Bay. They are sailing "to a world that others might have missed." "Ride, Captain, Ride" is not strictly a musical interpretation of the Noah legend. However, it can be interpreted as a mysterious expedition by adventurous people looking for a better world.

IKE AND TINA TURNER

Jennifer Heftler
Valley Stream, New York

Q. *How did you get started?*

Ike: When I was six years old I played on an old piano in a church lady's house. She would let me play if I would cut wood for her in return. At that time, I didn't really know what a piano was. All I knew was that when I pushed down on the keys it made a sound that I liked. After picking out a few notes to "Blues in the Night," and other tunes that were popular at the time, I started to beg my mother to buy me one of my own! When school was out that year I came home with a re-

port card full of good grades. I walked in the house and there it was . . . a new piano and she said it was all mine! This was the real beginning of my career.

Tina: I was going to night clubs with my sister. Ike was working at one that we used to go to all the time. Well, I used to ask him to let me sing . . . he'd say "O.K.," but never call me to the stage. One night he was playing organ and the drummer put a microphone in front of my sister for her to sing. She said, "No," and I took the microphone and started singing. Ike was shocked! He finished playing the tune, and called me on stage. I did several numbers with them that night . . . later I joined the group.

GOLD RECORDS

Lulu Miller
New York, New York

Q. *Where did the idea of a Gold Record first get started and how does the thing work? What does the artist actually get? Is it really a Gold Record, what is it made of?*

A. A Gold Record is given to recording artists who sell a million singles or $1,000,000 worth of LP's. To reach $1,000,000 in LP sales a recording artist generally has to sell 250,000 albums. Going back to the early days of recording, the first million-selling record was a 1919 disc for the Victor label consisting of two tunes, "Dardanella" and "I'm Forever Blowing Bubbles." The artist was Ben Selvin, a band leader-violinist.

Henry Brief, Executive Director, Recording Industry Association of America, Inc.: About Gold Records — as best we can learn, the first gold record award ever made was presented to Glenn Miller for his single "Chattanooga Choo Choo." Others began using the idea, and ultimately people started handing them out so promiscuously, and with so little basis in fact, that they began to be widely suspect both inside and outside the industry. As a consequence, Recording Industry Association of America inaugurated its certification program in 1958 in an attempt to salvage the reputation of the award by setting up a valid certification procedure. For the most part, companies use a metal mother which they plate with gold.

The Beatles have won more gold record awards than anyone else.

JAMES BROWN

Christopher Mil
Springfield, Massachusetts

Q. *How old were you when you started out?*

James: I started singing for nickels at about six years old, as a shoeshine boy in Augusta, Georgia. I didn't get a chance to finish the seventh grade, but I made it. I made it because He believed in me — because I had honesty and dignity and sincerity, and I wanted to be somebody. The other day I was talking to the kids — stay in school and don't be a dropout. Education is the answer. Know what you are talking about. Be qualified. Be ready. Then you will have a chance. Be ready, know what you are doing. You know in Augusta, Georgia, I used to shine shoes on the steps of the radio station, WDRW. But today, I own that radio station.

You know what that is? That's black power. It's not in violence. It's in knowing what you are talking about. Being ready. Now, I say to you, I'm your brother. I know where it's at. I've been there. I am not using my imagination. I am talking from experience. I have picked cotton. I did everything. I was nine years old before I got my first pair of underwear from a store. All my clothes were made from sacks and things like that. You know what I'm talking about. This is our language. We know where it's at. But I know that I had to make it. I had to have the determination to go on, and my determination was to be somebody.

Alan M. Leeds, James Brown Productions: Mr. Brown was singing and dancing for nickels in the Augusta area at the age of six. Soldiers at nearby Fort Gordon would gather around the young Brown and become fascinated with his ability. Brown has told us that his only major influence among other entertainers was singer-saxist Louis Jordan, whose Tympanny Five were probably the most popular black musical group in the forties. Brown sang popular songs of that era including those of Jordan, Charles Brown, and the Treniers. One such tune was "Caldonia" which he recorded for Smash Records in 1964.

The only way the street performing helped him towards the fantastic career he has now is through experience. He was singing from hunger and

learned how to control and develop an audience. In a sense he was conning people out of their change so he could get shoes on his feet. His tremendous sense of showmanship and fantastic "hold" on an audience today can be attributed to this background. However, between the times on the streets and becoming a music star, Brown served two years in a reformatory in Georgia, played semi-pro baseball and football, and had three professional matches as a boxer. His first professional date was in late 1954 when he formed the Swanees, a Gospel group that became Brown's Famous Flames in 1955. His first recording was "Please Please Please" in January 1956.

MARY TRAVERS
(PETER, PAUL, AND MARY)

Jennifer Heftler
Valley Stream, New York

Q. *How did Mary Travers get started?*

A. Mary Travers is a tall, willowy blonde with a tall, willowy voice, who's been singing folk songs since she was in a kindergarten class taught by Charity Bailey. "I went to a lot of New York progressive schools," she explains, "where there's plenty of art and music and the like."

Born in Louisville, Kentucky, in 1937, Mary came to New York with her parents, both newspaper people, after a Louisville paper went out of business. She loved to sing in her high school

chorus, "Where I could really make a lot of noise, but now Peter has to quiet me down." Mary sang with teenage folk groups that made it to Carnegie Hall twice and cut three records. "But I never dared sing on my own," she says. "I was scared to death."

A spot in the chorus of *The Next President* with Mort Sahl lasted only two weeks of Broadway's 1957 season, and Mary pretty much closes her career on the stage with this vehicle.

She took a series of jobs in literary and advertising agencies, utilizing her secondary talents. During high school she had a story published in *Seventeen,* and later she studied for a year at the Art Institute of New York. In 1961 in the Village, she met Paul Stookey and Peter Yarrow, formed a trio, and their first LP, *Peter, Paul, and Mary* was released.

GETTING WORDS TO SONGS

Vicki Hyatt
Santa Ana, California

Q. *Where can I get all the songs and all the words to the oldies but goodies 1963–1970 in a book?*

A. No one book has all the pop hits, words, and music, for those years. However, there are a few sources you can turn to. You can try to get back issues of the *Hit Parader*, Charlton Publications, Inc., Charlton Building, Derby, Connecticut. It publishes monthly collections of pop song lyrics. Along with this, Charlton Publications puts out the *Hit Parader Year Books* which are annual collections of the top selling songs, and they have the lyrics printed in them. If Charlton doesn't have any back copies of the year books you might try second-hand magazine dealers. You can also go to your record store and check up on anthology type LP's. Often there are discs of hits of each year. Ask your record dealer about that and also look up *Schwann's,* the authoritative catalogue of records, which lists them. If you are looking for the words and the music, there are many song folios, or song collections put out. Contact Charles Hansen Publications and they can give you information on those folios which contain the lyrics and music of the top hits for the years you want. The address is: Charles Hansen Publications, 250 Carol Place, Moonachie, New Jersey. You can also contact G. Schirmer (4 East 49th Street, New York, New York 10017) regarding sheet music pop hits through the years.

JOHNNY CASH

Rosie Johnson
Greenville, Ohio
Q. *Do you like rock music?*
Johnny: Yes.

Deborah Williams
Red Fox, Kentucky
Q. *Do you like black singers as well as white? Or is it based on what they sing?*
Johnny: I like a song that tells a story — no matter who sings it.

Tom Quickle
Loudenville, Ohio
Q. *How could I get started in the music business? I play country and western music, and people say that I sound a lot like you. I know I couldn't get as good as you, but could you give me some tips on how I could get started?*

Johnny: You have to have strong determination and a desire. Try out in your own hometown first. Participate in local talent shows, benefits, etc., where you are known, and work from there. It's hard work but you can do anything you really want to do.

Q. *What clothes would you suggest?*

Johnny: I wear what I'm comfortable in.

Elsie Haipee
Springfield, Ohio

Q. *How far did you go in school?*

Johnny: 12th grade.

Q. *How old is your son? Why don't you bring him on TV?*

Johnny: He's one year old. He hasn't asked to be on yet.

Q. *How old is Johnny Cash?*

A. The country singer-songwriter Johnny Cash was born on February 26, 1932. This makes him 38. He was born in Kingsland, Arkansas ("just a wide place in the road"). He was the fourth of seven children of a cotton farmer, hard hit by the big Depression of the 1930's. As a boy, Johnny picked cotton.

Q. *Who taught Johnny to play and sing?*

A. Johnny is pretty much a self-taught singer and guitarist. He grew up with hard work — and singing. He remembers singing hymns with his family almost constantly while doing chores. Then, too, his brother Roy had a four-piece country music combo when Johnny was a boy. Roy's band played at dances and over the radio. By the time he was 12 years old, Johnny wrote songs. During high school he sang on station KLCN in Blytheville, Arkansas. When the Korean war broke out in the 1950's, 22-year-old Johnny Cash enlisted in the Air Corps, and was sent to Germany. There he continued his writing, and sent in some of his songlike poetry to the army paper, *Stars and Stripes*. In his second year in Germany, he was lonely and wandered into a music store and bought a guitar. With this instrument, he started to practice and learn rudimentary chords.

Mauren Brinkman
Hamilton, Ohio
Q. *How many children does Johnny Cash have?*
A. He has three girls, Kathy, Cindy, and Tara. In Spring '70, the Cash's got an addition — a boy, John Carter Cash.

Steve Ash
Willow Wood, Ohio
Q. *I am proud to say that I watch* The Johnny Cash Show *every Wednesday at* 9 P.M. *I think he's the greatest singer there is in country music. I would like to know how he got started.*
A. After being released from the Air Force, Johnny Cash got married. He fumbled around looking for a way to support his wife and himself. For a while, he worked as a door-to-door salesman selling appliances in Memphis. He wasn't a cracking success at it. Somehow he got the feeling that he could make it in pop music. He started to meet with Luther Perkins, who played guitar, and Marshall Grant, a bass player. They got together at night, rehearsing and talking about country music. Finally, Johnny and his "Tennessee Two"

gathered up enough courage to approach Sam Phillips of Sun Records for an audition. A quick-witted excountry music disc jockey, Phillips was the man who discovered Presley. He ran Sun Records. His voice shaking with fright, Cash started to sing in the Sun studio. When Cash got to a song he himself wrote, "Hey, Porter," Phillips stood up, and turned on the recording equipment. In that one take, the first side of Cash's record debut was made. Later, that one and a romantic weeper, "Cry, Cry, Cry" became Cash's first singles release in June 1955. It climbed pretty high on the country music charts. The Johnny Cash story was starting.

Deborah Williams
Red Fox, Kentucky

Q. *What does Johnny Cash think about teenagers taking drugs?*

A. The tall, muscular, craggy-faced star is very much against drugs. In fact, on his ABC-TV program, he has publicly and eloquently told of the dangers of taking drugs because: "I've been there." In the early part of his career, Johnny was running around like a hyperactive possum. His schedule of personal appearances, recording-sessions, publicity interviews took a toll on his muscular physique. He started doing what many other show people were doing. He started to take pep pills to keep him going ("bennies," benzedrine) and tranquilizers to go to sleep. By 1967, he was getting very rocky. Several times, he didn't show up for scheduled concerts. Pop promoters were marking him "lousy." He was going steadily downhill. In 1968, the newspapers headlined the story of Johnny Cash being arrested in El Paso, Texas. While getting off a plane, Federal narcotics agents took him into custody. They searched him and found more than 1,000 pills on him. The country star pleaded guilty to the charge and was fined. Of his drug days, Cash says: "I was walking death. I used to take up to 100 pills a day. I don't know why they didn't kill me. Any doctor would tell you it would. I would play one against the other — pep pills to pep me up, and tranquilizers to calm me down."

Rick Dokken
Garden Grove, California

Q. *Is there a new album out with all Johnny*

Cash's hits such as "A Boy Named Sue," and "Folsom Prison"?

A. Columbia recently released a deluxe two-record set consisting of 20 of Johnny's big songs and records, *The World of Johnny Cash*. However, the two songs you refer to are not on it. But a good deal of his work is there.

Q. *I would like to know why Johnny Cash has been writing all the songs about prisons. Is it because he feels sorry for the guys there?*

A. In 1955, to kill time, Johnny Cash dropped into a movie house and saw a film, *Inside the Walls of Folsom Prison*. It inspired him to write the song "Folsom Prison Blues." Released in 1956, the record became Johnny Cash's first smash hit. Since then he has been giving of his time and talent to entertain prisoners. He started doing prison shows in the late '50's. He believes that prisoners are great audiences, and obviously feels sympathetic to their problems. It was Cash who thought up the idea of taping an album before an audience of convicts titled *Johnny Cash at Folsom Prison*.

Angel Owens
West Union, South Carolina

Q. *Was Johnny Cash ever in prison?*

A. Yes. In the notes to his Columbia album, *Johnny Cash at Folsom Prison* (1968) Cash wrote: "I have been behind bars a few times. Sometimes of my own volition, sometimes involuntarily. Each time I felt the same feeling of kinship with my fellow prisoners."

Daffany Null
Vandali, Missouri
Q. *Is it true that Johnny's first wife was black?*
A. Johnny's first wife was an Italian girl, Vivian Liberto of San Antonio, Texas. They had known each other for four years prior to their marriage. They were wed in a Catholic church, August 7, 1954. The story that Johnny Cash was married to a black girl was circulated by the Ku Klux Klan. Later on, Johnny got a divorce and married June Carter.

Sherill Martin
North Tonawanda, New York
Q. *Is the Carter Family really June Carter's mother and sisters?*
A. Yes. Johnny Cash's second wife is country singer June Carter. They were married in Nash-

ville on March 1, 1968. June has cut records with her sisters Helen and Anita. The girls have also recorded with their mother, Mama Maybelle. As such they are known as country music's "first family." June met Johnny when the Carter Family went on tour with *The Johnny Cash Show.* You can hear Johnny and the Carter Family together in an album of religious songs composed by Johnny, *The Holy Land.*

Q. *When Johnny Cash isn't doing his show, does he still live in Nashville?*

A. Not exactly. He spends a good deal of his non-working hours at his home in Hendersonville, Tennessee, not far from Nashville. He lives in a sprawling home set on a cliff overlooking a lake. His mother and father live nearby in a house that Johnny bought for them. For relaxation, Johnny farms a vegetable garden. "I can work in that garden all morning and I'm ready to come in here and make the show in the afternoon," he says.

Roger de Foss
Billings, Montana

Q. *How many awards has Johnny Cash won over these past few years?*

A. You'd need a good sized pick-up truck to carry all of Johnny Cash's awards. He's won more than 80. These consist of more than 5 Grammy's (given by the National Academy of Recording Arts and Sciences), music business polls, trade paper citations, magazine awards, country music awards. Several of his plaques come from abroad. The country music star has acquired six gold records so far.

JAY AND THE AMERICANS

Robert Itkin
West Orange, New Jersey
Q. Who's considered the best rock drummer?
Jay and The Americans: Jim Capaldi [Traffic].
Q. Who's considered the best lead guitarist?
Jay And A: Eric Clapton.
Q. The best bass guitarist?
Jay and A: Jack Casady [Jefferson Airplane].
Q. The best organist?
Jay And A: Steve Winwood.
Q. The best vocalist in terms of voice quality?
Jay and A: Paul McCartney.

The Association

THE ASSOCIATION

Linda Torok
New Brunswick, New Jersey
Q. *What is your favorite song?*
Brian Cole: To name one would mean to omit a hundred.
Terry Kirkman: I really don't have a favorite song; more like favorite compositions. Like Respeghi's "Pines and Fountains of Rome," and the things Gil Evans did with Mile's, "Sketches of Spain." Those are things that caught hold of me at an early age and pushed me on. As far as songs are concerned, there are certain ones I look at from a craftsmanship point of view, like "Dino's Song," by Dino Valenti, which is a remarkable piece of work. He also wrote "Let's Get Together," which is, to me, an almost perfect song — it has a great chronology, all the words have meaning, the alliteration is perfect, not to mention the melody. There are a lot of old standards that are flawlessly put together. Of course, the language was different so we don't respond to them anymore. In the middle of an era you can't see what is going to become representative of that era. For example, Matt Dennis, during the thirties and forties, wrote some of the most incredible songs . . . like "Cottage for Sale." A classic. I would suggest that only about one per cent of the people reading this will even know who he is. Sinatra, Bennet, Sammy Davis, all say, hands down, that

Matt Dennis was one of the finest song stylists *ever*. But I think the test of the era will be to see which songs survive. Joni Mitchell's will be around for a long time because they can be sung for twenty years; they have a type of introspective approach to music that makes them timeless.

James Yester: I really like a lot of different *kinds* of music. I have a favorite classical piece, a favorite tune, like "Cherish," different things like that. I feel a lot of musical influence in the kinds of things I like to listen to and the things I fool around with when I'm rehearsing. They come from two places, by the way. One, the church, believe it or not, because I grew up in the Catholic church singing in choirs and glee clubs, and singing solemn high mass in Latin. As a matter of fact, the other day I was playing around with liturgy which has the grooviest melodies . . . and singing an occasional Gregorian chant in the shower.

Gina Fasanella
Ardsley, New York

Q. *How do you feel with no top forty hits for a while?*

Jules Alexander: Well, pretty good, to tell you the truth. I'm not saying there is anything too much wrong with having a hit going for you, except that when you do, you tend to chase yourself. And you try to blast those hits away, and push them. But without hits you obviously don't have to do that. We're not trying NOT to make some hits, but we're not pushing it that hard. We always had great album sales, so we're not too worried. Our performances still sell out wherever we go, so nobody's worried. In fact I don't really mind it a bit.

Brian Cole: Make no mistake, singles are really neat, and it's nice to know they are playing one of your things on the radio, and have people hear it and tell you, but it's just as neat to go into a place after not having a hit for a year and a half, and have ten thousand people turn out and dig ya. It often happens, believe it or not; another group with a single going will play the same city and not draw at all. People come to see us because we're a performing group, and they like our work. But if you are talking about money, singles are where some of your money is, not to mention personal satisfaction. But someone right behind you can put out a single that has hiss and scratch and no meaning to the lyrics, use three chords over and over, and sell twice as many as something you did which was better. The vagaries of the market are so unexplainable and complex that I don't think there is anybody in the world who really knows. Although there are about one hundred thousand who say they know.

Terry Kirkman: In a sense, not having a hit is kind of a relief, in that it gives us a tremendous amount of artistic freedom. We are already established, and I don't think we are pursuing, from a contrived point of view, the top forty market. The top forty market for an adult artist seems to be geared to a very low age bracket. You have to avoid certain images and words. It's the difference between a bubble gum song and a Dylan or Joni Mitchell song.

James Yester: To say it isn't disappointing would be a lie, because it is.

MONEY! MONEY! MONEY!

Gary Snyderman
Plymouth Meeting, Pennsylvania

Q. *Pop concerts seem to be popping up all over the place. What do pop stars and groups make for a concert?*

A. The concert field, once dominated by Bach, Beethoven, and Brahms, has now become a million-dollar offshoot of the pop business. You'll find almost as many pop concerts as frisbees. This is true despite isolated incidents of violence and drugs for sale openly. The concerts are everywhere — inside vast college auditoriums, alongside dusty auto-tracks, on hillsides, in inner-city parks, even in concert halls. Pop stars and groups earn a lot of money on them, depending on their "names," and how many hits they've recently had on the Top Ten. Some so-called "super groups," demand a flat $25,000 for a single concert. Some lesser groups with "name value" earn much less. Last summer, the New York Rock Ensemble, which mixes rock and the classics, reported that their "college concert price is averaging $3500."

Some pop groups are even promoting their own concerts. They take 90 per cent of the box office income and offer 10 per cent to the local concert promoter. Pop concerts are not sure-fire bonanzas. The printing of handbills, radio advertising, publicity, placards, do not automatically result in a pop concert success. Not long ago, the highly publicized English rock group, the Ginger Baker Airforce, had to cancel a Madison Square Garden concert because of poor advance sale.

Sometimes top groups donate their services free of charge for causes they believe in. Recently, a big pop peace festival was produced at New York's Shea Stadium, the home of the baseball Mets. The artists — Creedence Clearwater Revival, The Rascals, Paul Simon, Steppenwolf, Dionne Warwick, Al Cooper-Richie, Miles Davis, the cast of *Hair* — played and sang, without charge, from 10 A.M. to midnight on a stage erected near second base. Some of the funds went to antiwar organizations. Some were donated to senators and congressmen who have taken a strong anti-Viet Nam war position, and to assist them in today's costly election campaigns.

Q. *What did pop stars make at Woodstock?*

A. As they say in show business, the controversial Woodstock Festival, on the slopes of a dairy farm in upstate New York, had an enormous "nut."

That is, costs ran very high. The cost for talent alone over a three-day period went to $250,000. The money was divided among 29 acts, including The Jefferson Airplane, The Who, Joan Baez, Arlo Guthrie, John Sebastian, Country Joe and the Fish, Richie Havens, Crosby, Stills and Nash, Jimi Hendrix, Sly and the Family Stone. The pop stars are also sharing in the record royalties. The Woodstock album has become a fantastic multimillion dollar success. More than 1,000,000 of the costly three LP packages were sold by the summer's end of 1970. The film version, *Woodstock*, has grossed more than $5,000,000, as of August, 1970.

Q. *On the average, how much would a group make for a one-night stand at New York's Madison Square Garden?*

Sid Bernstein, famed concert promoter who presented The Beatles in the U.S.A.: If you're talking about a pop group starring by itself, a top group would make $40,000 to $60,000 for a one-night stand at Madison Square Garden. I presented Blood, Sweat and Tears recently at the Garden and I paid them $50,000. Generally, the deal consists of a guarantee plus percentage of the box office. Another time, I presented Joan Baez in a concert at the Garden which holds approximately 20,000. I offered her $20,000 plus a percentage. She said, "Sid, I'll play it for you for $5,000, but you'll have to charge $2 admission, no higher." So I charged $2 admission and we broke even. But I had the pleasure of presenting a great artist in an interesting atmosphere. It was a marvelous evening.

Q. *How much does a top pop group or star make at Fillmore East?*

Sid Bernstein: Usually a top group will make $20,000 for a weekend ($5,000 a show) at Fillmore East. This would consist of four shows, two a day on Friday and Saturday. It's a place that groups like to play. It has a tradition and a great atmosphere. (Some pop groups make $2,000 at Fillmore East, some even less.)

Q. *What do pop stars and groups have to pay out of their earnings for business expenses?*

Sid Bernstein: On the average a pop group has to pay 10 per cent to a booking agency, who arranges for dates and jobs. Then they have to pay 10 to 15 per cent to their personal managers who oversee all the business and professional strategy. Other expenses include two road managers (at about $125 a week each) who take care of travelling schedules, luggage, hotel reservations, and musical equipment.

MICHAEL PARKS

Pam Bush
Salem, Ohio

Q. *Could you tell me as much as you can about Michael (Bronson) Parks?*

A. Michael Parks rose to fame as a sensitive man on a motorcycle in NBC-TV's program *Then Came Bronson*. The show was cancelled in the summer of 1970. He still records for MGM Records. He has been described as young, restless, bright, strong, impatient, soft-spoken, and outspoken. Some say he is difficult, impossible to work with. He is not the boy next door.

While he portrayed a character who roamed the highways and dusty sideroads on his motorcycle, fearless and unafraid, in real life he is afraid of some things. He's reluctant to fly. For a guest shot on *The Ed Sullivan Show* he insisted on taking a three-day cross country railroad trip rather than a six-hour flight.

Parks was born April 24 in Corona, California, in a time of uncertainty and rootlessness. "Home" for the family of two boys and three girls was often an empty warehouse, a garage, or temporary camp site. When his dad wasn't working as a truck driver, the family sifted and sacked oak leaf mold for sale to nurseries.

At fourteen, Michael was on his own. He attended twenty-one schools, never graduating from high school, yet attended junior college. An English teacher in northern California gave him an early appreciation for books which has never faded. He is an avid reader, and once had a personal library of over 2,000 books. The entire collection was stolen, a loss on which Parks prefers not to elaborate. However, he is not reluctant to discuss his early wanderings, which took him to virtually all parts of his home state.

As a kid on the road he was "always looking for something." To eat, he drove trucks, fought fires, baled hay, picked crops and, at one point, upholstered caskets.

Parks' career as an actor began in San Francisco and Sacramento. In Hermosa Beach, a few miles south of Los Angeles, he tried out for, and landed, one of the lead roles in a local production of *Compulsion*. A talent agent, Jack Fields, saw his performance and got him a guest role in the daytime improvisational series *Day in Court* on the ABC-TV Network. Other television appearances followed, and then motion pictures. He has since starred in such features as *Wild Seed, Bus Riley's Back in Town, The Idol, Channing,* and *The Bible.* In the latter, he was seen as Adam.

Q. *Is he married? If so, does he have any children?*
A. Michael is married and the father of three. A few years ago, he and his brunette wife, Kay, settled in a rural community in Ventura County, commuting distance from Los Angeles. The children are Patricia, Stephanie, and Jim.

Shortly before the start of production on *Then Came Bronson,* Mike added a new dimension to his career by recording an album of country songs, *Closing the Gap.* His LP, *Long Lonesome Highway,* hit the best-seller lists.

GETTING STARTED AS A SINGER

Jennifer Heftler
Valley Stream, New York

Q. *How can I get started as a singer?*

Theodore Bikel, folk singer: You don't get started, you just sing. Eventually, if you are good enough, someone is going to hear what you do and like it. This is a society which won't tolerate your doing something well without forcing you to accept money for it.

Q. *Would you encourage your son or daughter to become a singer?*

Bikel: I wouldn't discourage them.

THE CHARTS

Tommy Miles
Wollaston, Massachusetts

Q. *You hear a lot about the Top Ten. Who decides which records go on the charts? When did these charts originate, and how are they put together?*

Irv Lichtman, Editor of *Cash Box*: In the final analysis, of course, it's the record buyer who determines which recordings — singles (45's) or albums (LP's) — will reach Top Ten status. A staff of statistical personnel works with reports obtained from retail outlets, through forms and, for last minute results, telephone calls. This tally, from all key record markets in the U.S., is added up, based on a weighting system based on the importance to record sales of each market. *Cash*

Box began a chart listing shortly after its formation in 1942.

Andy Tomko, Director of Charts, *Billboard*: *Billboard* started record charts back in the early 1940's, at which time we ran three separate singles charts — bestselling in stores, most played on radio, and most played in juke boxes. In the late 1950's, the charts were combined into a single chart listing the top 100 singles of the week. In the early 1960's, the present "Hot 100" chart evolved and has continued to this time.

None of our charts is based on actual sales figures, but rather a relative sales response from dealers (how well he is selling a particular record compared to all others he is selling). We have no fix as to how many records were sold to attain a particular position on the chart. Also, since each week is usually different as to sales in the field, it is very possible that a Top Ten record's sales would vary during the year according to how sales are, the season of the year, and the like. However, it is generally accepted that a record attaining Top Ten will have a cumulative sales of from 600,000 on up. The chart, however, is not based on cumulative sales, only a one-week spread, so this is not to say that a record must sell 600,000 in one week to reach Top Ten.

WHO'S THE "BEST"?

Robert Itkin
West Orange, New Jersey

The answers to the following questions were

gathered by Stu Ginsberg, Publicity Director of Capitol Records, East Coast Division. He prefaced the answers with this note: "I've asked all our producers here, and they all say (and I agree) that you cannot ask so general a question as to who is the best anything. I will answer the five questions with the various names given me."

Q. *Who's considered the best rock drummer?*
A. Ginger Baker, Ringo Starr.
Q. *Who's considered the best lead guitarist?*
A. George Harrison, Eric Clapton.
Q. *Who's considered the best bass guitarist?*
A. Paul McCartney.
Q. *The best organist?*
A. Brian Auger, Jimmy McGriff, Stevie Winwood.
Q. *The best vocalist in terms of voice quality?*
A. There are hundreds.

l. to r.—Steve Winwood, Rick Grech, Ginger Baker, Eric Clapton, of Cream

HENRY MANCINI

Philip Balbi
Miami, Florida

Q. *How did you get interested in music? At what age? What was your first instrument, and how much did it cost?*

Henry: I was coerced at the age of eight into playing the piccolo by my dad, who was a semi-professional flute player. I have no idea as to the cost of that first piccolo. It was brought over from Italy by my dad and was probably quite old by the time it got to me. I didn't have any real interest in music until I was thirteen when I began to play the piano. This opened up enormous possibilities for me, since I was always interested in harmony and chords, rather than just the single melodic line available to the flute.

Q. *What are some of the good things and some of the bad things in today's pop music scene?*

Henry: One of the really good things happening to today's pop music scene is the high level of performance and arranging by the new people. Vocal harmonies are extremely well written and well performed. The same applies to the instrumentalists. On the minus side, I would say that an inordinate number of contemporary melodies seem to sound alike. How many times can you use the first two bars of "Little Green Apples"?

Q. *How do you go about writing a Hollywood film score?*

Henry: (Winner of two Oscars for Best Song: "Moon River" and "Days of Wine and Roses," and another Oscar for the complete film score for *Breakfast at Tiffany's*.) To simplify an involved process: Sometimes I am called into a film at the preshooting stage and I am able to read the script. However, just as often I am called after the entire film has been shot. I prefer not to see the day-to-day shooting. I feel it is a waste of time, since a great deal of what is actually shot ends up on the cutting room floor. My first discussions are with the producer and/or director. An exchange of ideas is very necessary at this point. We view the film together and mutually make final decisions as to where the music is going to be placed. I then view the film as many as eight to ten times until I am really familiar with every sequence.

During this time, the music editor, who acts as my assistant, makes up timing sheets of each sequence in minute detail from the beginning of each sequence to be scored to the end. This is my guide while I am writing, since after these initial screenings I rarely look at the film again until the scoring sessions.

Normally the composing, orchestrating, and copying of a score, in my case, takes from four to six weeks. The actual recording for a normal length picture averages four to six sessions of three hours each. The music tracks are then combined with all of the visual and other sound aspects of the film. This process is called dubbing, from which the final release print is made.

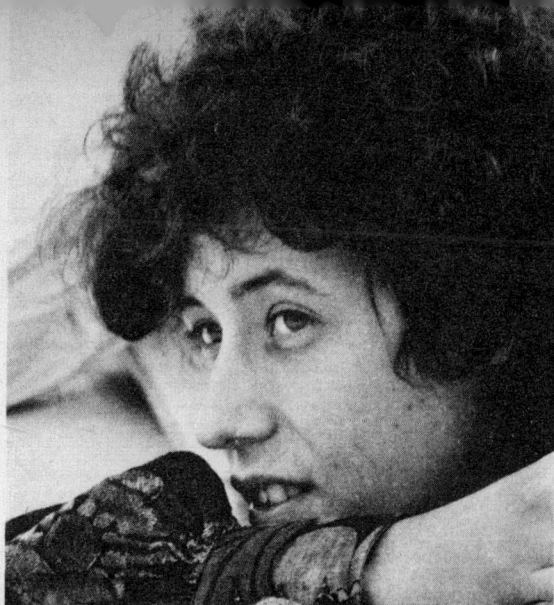

ARLO GUTHRIE

Greg Romano
Watertown, Connecticut
Q. *Before* Alice's Restaurant *became a hit did you have any movies or records out?*
Arlo: No movies, but a record was out.
Q. *Did you enjoy making* Alice's Restaurant?
Arlo: Yes.
Q. *Do you compose all your own songs?*
Arlo: Most of them.

John Scott
Armonk, New York
Q. *Are you going to continue your musical career now that you're married to Jackie Hyde?*
Arlo: Yes I am.

Q. *Do you consider yourself a folk or a rock singer?*

Arlo: Just a singer.

Q. *What is your favorite type music?*

Arlo: All music.

Q. *What have you learned from your father [the late, legendary, Woody Guthrie, folk singer/song writer] and your father's songs?*

Arlo: Plenty.

Q. *Is there going to be a film based on your father's life and are you going to be in it?*

Arlo: Yes, there will be a film. Don't know if I'll be in it. [Hollywood has bought the rights to *Bound for Glory*, the autobiography of the late Woody Guthrie. He wrote more than 1,000 songs, including "This Land Is Your Land." His songs of the '30's and '40's reflected a populist spirit — Guthrie was devoted to the common man and to radical reform. He used folk music forms to write about current events. Arlo Guthrie's father died in 1967 at the age of 55. His last few years were spent in a hospital. Arlo was shown visiting a hospital in *Alice's Restaurant.*]

ANDY WILLIAMS

Mark Sneddon
Columbus Falls, Montana

Q. *Who is the producer and arranger for Andy Williams?*

A. Big companies like Columbia have salaried "house producers" on staff, each of whom handle a number of artists or groups. If an artist doesn't get along with a certain record producer, or isn't happy artistically with his musical approach, he may ask for somebody else. Sometimes singers and groups change producers because they may want a certain sound or style. Sometimes pop stars go outside the company and choose freelance producers. It's the same with arrangers. There's no fixed deal by which an artist is locked to a particular arranger. Often an artist switches to a "hot" arranger who has had a streak of hits. For the record, here are the credits for recent LP's cut by Andy Williams:

Get Together — Jerry Fuller, producer; Al Capps, arranger

Happy Heart — Jerry Fuller, producer; Al Capps, arranger

Raindrops Keep Fallin' on My Head —Dick Glasser, producer; Al Capps, arranger.

MELANIE

Mathew Friedman
Los Angeles, California

Q. *Did you ever take music lessons?*

Melanie: I never took lessons.

Q. *How did you get started? Your first professional date? How much did you get paid?*

Melanie: Walked around a lot of buildings, walked down a lot of streets. All the buildings and all the streets culminated in Peter Schekeryk's office [a freelance record producer]. My first professional date was at the Quay in Seabright, New Jersey, for $20.

Q. *Do you mind if people come to see you backstage after a concert?*

Melanie: There's no reason why I can't see the people who want to see me. I mean I'm not the Beatles. They're not going to tear me apart or anything.

THE WHO

D. S. Fenichel
Livingston, New Jersey

Q. *So far, approximately how many copies of* Tommy *have been sold?*

Nancy Lewis, American representative of The Who: Sales of *Tommy* (Decca) have passed 750,000 by the end of 1970. Actually the record has had an amazing life. It is still selling almost two years after it was released in June 1969. When released, the album got a lot of attention as the first rock opera. Sales dropped off in the spring of 1970. Then it picked up in the summer of 1970 assisted by The Who's presentation of *Tommy* at the Metropolitan Opera House in Lincoln Center, and a road tour of the U.S.

Rita Rodriguez
Kansas City, Missouri
Q. *Did you first start out as a high school band?*
Roger Daltrey: Yes, we started out as the equivalent of a high school band in England. We weren't in a school band but we had a band in school. We were about 15 years old. We were called The Detours. To go back a minute, John Entwistle was in the official school band as a french horn player. Six of us were in the Detours including Peter Townshend and John. In 1963 we became a quartet and changed our name to The High Numbers. At that time Keith Moon replaced our regular drummer. Keith simply jumped on stage one night and took over. We didn't do too much in those days — played small clubs for little money. In 1964 we became The Who.

Andrea Goldman
Concord, California
Q. *Which do you like better, performing or writing?*
Peter: [He does most of the writing for The Who]. Performing is very important to us. We'd never stop performing. We believe strongly in audience contact.
Q. *Do you plan to write any more operas?*
Peter: There's always a possibility. Right now I'm finishing songs for a studio album. I'm not concentrating on a new opera now. However, *Tommy* seems to have a life of its own. The Royal Canadian Ballet Company of Montreal has produced *Tommy* as a ballet. And England's Young Vic is doing its own theatre version.

Q. *Did you enjoy performing at the Met?*

John: Yes, but it was exhausting for we did two shows in one day. We were ready to drop after the first show. Each show took over two hours. [*Tommy* is the story in music and lyrics of a blind, deaf, and dumb boy. He becomes a pinball wizard and a big attraction, and a preacher of sermons. He is introduced by a disc jockey and preceded by gospel groups. Later he opens a kind of camp. *Tommy* was produced at the famed Met not by the Metropolitan Opera House but by The Who]. *The New York Times* wrote in a picture caption: WHO'S AT THE MET? THE WHO, THAT'S WHO.

THE TOP GROUPS:
HOW MUCH DO THEY MAKE?

M. Strehlow
Ottawa, Kansas

Q. *How much money do groups such as The Guess Who, The Rolling Stones, and Jefferson Airplane make on the average per year?*

A. Only their accountants know for sure. But music business veterans say that top groups earn about $1,000,000 and up. This income flows in from: (a) records, (b) song royalties, (c) TV guest shots, (d) personal appearances, (e) films. A hot group that climbs swiftly into the top money orbit can make more money than they know what to do with.

Consider the Grand Funk Railroad, which records for Capitol. In the short space of a year, it has become richer than the Pennsylvania Railroad. According to their press agents, the group has already grossed $1,500,000 on its first two Capitol albums. The second, *Grand Funk,* is an RIAA certified $1-million seller, and their current album *Closer to Home,* is joining it. It was ranked among the Top Ten best sellers in the nation the day it was released.

Grand Funk will pocket more than $300,000 during two months of summer appearances, feeding into a total gross estimated at $2 million plus for 1970. And even that figure is exclusive of record publishing royalties, according to Grand Funk Railroad's manager and producer, Terry Knight.

Grand Funk Railroad debuted as an opening

act at the Atlanta Pop Festival. They played for free. Now, as a multimillion dollar corporation, they carry 12 full-time employees on the payrolls, and tote three tons of equipment on concert dates. Knight, plus a road manager, two equipment handlers, two sound technicians, and four private pilots join Grand Funk on dates.

The gear, including a 2,000-watt full-stereophonic sound system utilizing 12 microphones and 200-watt monitor system, moves by a C-46 cargo plane. Personnel swing from stop-to-stop via a Lear Jet leased by GFR Enterprises, Ltd., the Grand Funk corporation.

Regardless of what a top group or star earns, it is not pure profit. There are countless behind-the-scenes expenses: high income tax, social security deductions, publicity expenses, clothes, arrangers' and choreographers' fees, travel expenses, lawyers' fees, accountants' fees.

MC 5

Mike Laird
Joplin, Missouri
Q. *Do you know anything of the lead singer, Robert Tyner, of the MC 5's background?*

Danny Fields of Atlantic Records for whom MC 5 records: Robert Tyner started out as a writer — a poet. Later he was approached to join a neighborhood rock band, which turned out to be the MC 5. The group grew up in the industrial suburbs of Detroit. Most of their parents and relatives worked in the giant auto plants — Ford, Chrysler, GM.

Q. Did he have another rock group before the MC 5?

Danny: No, not that I know of.

Q. Did any of the group have a previous group? I heard Wayne Kramer, lead guitarist, had a group, but I'd like to know.

Danny: I doubt it. But maybe there were little offshoot groups when they were 14, 15.

Q. What was the first single that the MC 5 put out?

Danny: They put out a record on their own consisting of two sides: "Borderline" and "Looking at You." Just a couple of hundred copies were pressed. There wasn't even a company label on them. Since then they have put out three albums including *Kick Out The Jams* (also released as a single disc), and an LP titled *Back in the USA*. In the summer of 1970, they toured Europe, England, Germany, and Holland. MC stands for Motor City. Some of their songs are: "Motor City is Burning," "The Human Being Lawnmower." Once Robert Tyner said, "It's a young planet. We're just starting to get out of the caves. What we try to say in our music is: Come out, have the whole planet, not just the room with the TV set."

THREE DOG NIGHT

Christine Clark
Springfield, Massachusetts
Q. *I think your group is really great. Your songs make me feel happy. What are your names?*
Three Dog Night: As you know, there are seven of us. We're Cory Wells, Danny Hutton, Chuck Negron. Also, Mike Alsup (lead guitar), Joe Schermie (bass, drums, guitar), Jim Greenspoon (keyboard, organ, piano, harpsichord), Floyd Sneed (percussion). There is no lead singer in the group — Cory, Chuck, and Danny sing lead at varying times.

Faith Stein
Maspeth, New York
Q. *What state do you live in?*
Three Dog Night: California.
Q. *How old are Danny and Cory?*
A. Danny Hutton was born September 10, 1943.
He's 27. Couldn't find out exactly how old Cory
is. But here are the vital statistics on each of them.

Danny	**Cory**
Birthdate —	Birthdate —
September 10	February 5
Hometown —	Hometown —
Buncrana, Ireland	Buffalo, New York
Hair — Brown	Hair — Blond
Eyes — Brown	Eyes — Blue

GARY PUCKETT

Penelope Coronel
Waianae, Hawaii

Q. *When did you get started?*

Gary: We got together, that's me and the Union Gap, in San Diego, California, in 1966. In 1967 we put out — better make that Columbia Records put out — four records of ours that sold over three quarters of a million copies apiece. The records were "Young Girl," "Lady Willpower," and "Woman, Woman," and "Over You." I was proud and the group was proud. Make that we're still proud. Only the Beatles had four gold records in one year. Considering that we were in the business one year when it happened, well, we're still proud.

Q. *What is your advice to me if I want to become a singer?*

Gary: It's hard to answer that question because everytime somebody opens his mouth to sing, it's a different sound, a different voice, a different attitude, and, obviously, a different degree of talent. The only advice I can give is don't copy style. You want to sing? Sing it the way your insides tell you to sing it. If you've got it inside, it'll come outside for everybody to hear. Carbon copies are just that, carbon copies. Just do it your way, not anybody's else's. If it's there, everyone will soon know about it.

Alden Solovy
Chicago, Illinois

Q. *Why does a group break up?*

Gary: Another tough question, because how can anyone generalize about personalities? My break with the Union Gap had nothing to do with personalities. I was always the singer and the Gap were always the musicians. The greatest, I might add. So, we broke up. I'm still a singer. They're still musicians. I'll do my thing. They'll do their thing. Only separately. Why did we break? The question still has to be answered. There are a few things I wanted to do professionally, areas of expression I felt were better catered to as a solo performer. Simple? Yes, simple. The Gap and I were friends, we are still friends, and we will remain friends. Our aims are similar. The only point to the break is these aims could be better realized by pursuing them from different directions. Too bad there's nothing juicy about it, no clashes, no hatreds. We LIKE each other! Sorry about that!

THE MONKEES:
WHERE ARE THEY NOW?

Karen Proeber
Franksville, Wisconsin

Q. *What instruments do each of the Monkees play?*

A. Mike Nesmith plays pedal steel guitar and six string guitar, and organ. Peter Tork plays piano, twelve-string bass, and five-string banjo. Davy Jones, tambourine, maracas. Mickey Dolenz plays drums and guitar. But it's no state secret that The Monkees have split. Once they were the hottest pop group in the music business. They were riding high with mounds of press clippings, a highly successful TV series, and half-a-dozen best-selling RCA albums. But they broke up over professional and personal differences. For a while they kept up with The Monkee thing. They star-

red in a wild surrealistic comedy satire film, *The Head;* the film didn't do too well at the box office. Mike Nesmith is still trying to make it as a recording artist on RCA. His group is called The First National Band. Peter Tork tried to get things going with his own group called Peter Tork and/or Release. But he seems to have lost heart and is rumored to be on a large farm in Connecticut. Things have been pretty quiet for Mickey Dolenz. Davy Jones, the lively little Englishman, has turned businessman. He is running a boutique, The Street. The operation is located in the basement of an exclusive, private Hollywood club called The Factory where show business people gather.

Cathy Ardolino
Brooklyn, New York
Q. *Does Davy Jones have a child?*
A. Linda and Davy Jones have one child.

DIANA ROSS

Evelyn Hughes
Washington, D.C.

Q. *Why did you leave The Supremes?*

Diana: I left The Supremes to try new things on my own. I look at it as part of the growth process.

Q. *Do you write your own songs?*

Diana: No. I have a group of top songwriters associated with Motown who write for me. They are Nick Ashford and Valerie Simpson, and Norman Whitfield. Also, a lot of my songs, some of my best, have been written by Smokey Robinson.

Maxine Fenner
Freeport, New York
Q. *Do you want to appear in any movies?*
Diana: Yes. That's one of the reasons I'm going it alone. I've had a lot of offers and I've turned down many roles. I just don't want to go into *any* movie. I don't want to move too fast and choose anything. I would like very much to play in a motion picture biography of the life of Billie Holiday. [Billie Holiday was one of the great jazz singers of all time. Born in Baltimore, Maryland, the beautiful, coppery-skinned vocalist led a troubled life. Even as a star, she faced two kinds of discrimination: (a) as a jazz artist and (b) because she was black. Also known as Lady Day, Billie's records are now collector's items. She also wrote several songs which are recorded quite often, "God Bless The Child," and "Fine and Mellow."]

Juanita Gillard
Sumter, South Carolina
Q. *What state do you live in?*
Diana: I now make my home in California.

Angel Owens
West Union, South Carolina
Q. *How did you become manager of the Jackson 5?*
Diana: I am not manager of the Jackson 5. I helped discover them. What happened was this: I heard them sing. I got very excited and told Berry Gordy, Jr., president of Motown Records, about them. He heard a demonstration record. Later, he went to see them perform in person. Well, he flipped. He told people that, "They're go-

117

ing to be one of the biggest groups in the business. No question about it." Well, he was right. Also, the Jackson family is a real nice family. Nice people.

Tony Pauline
Hazelton, Pennsylvania

Q. *How did Diana Ross get started?*

A. It all began in Detroit in 1960. Florence Ballard asked Mary Wilson to join her in establishing a pop singing group. Mary then asked Diana to be a part of it. All of them lived in a housing project — the Brewster Homes. Diana was around 16 then, thin and leggy, on the tomboyish side. She was one of six children. All of the girls were attending high school. The first name they sang under was The Primettes. Once underway, the girls sang everywhere — amateur shows, neighborhood affairs, school functions — anywhere they could showcase their talents.

While still in school, the girls heard of a new record firm just starting out — Motown Records. So they arranged for an audition. Berry Gordy, Jr., producer-owner, told them that they should come back after they had finished high school, which they did. At first, Gordy used them as choral background to other pop singers. They got about $2.50 per record. Later on, they persuaded Gordy to allow them to do a single. In 1964, they issued their first record as The Supremes (the name thought up by Florence). Their first hit was "Where Did Our Love Go?"

In mid-July 1967, the group was renamed — after much soul searching and debate: Diana

Ross and The Supremes. Reason? Diana was winning special acclaim as a standout glamour personality. Today, there's only one original Supreme left, Mary Wilson, who now works with Cindy Birdsong and Jean Terrell.

Eddie Dixon
Dayton, Ohio

Q. *How did Diana Ross learn to dance like that? Did she take lessons or did it come naturally?*

A. Sometimes called "the skinny Supreme," Diana Ross is lithe, small-boned. She moves easily and gracefully. When the Supremes started out, they developed little dance steps to give the trio some "eye-appeal." Much of this was similar to patterns they saw in other acts on TV. These patterns go back to the 1930's — the era of stage shows in moviehouses — to the days of the Ink Spots, the

119

Andrews Sisters, and the Mills Brothers. They consist of members of a group switching places, finger-snapping, moving from side to side, moving from three-across to single-file — all this is done while the song is being put over. Later on, when the Supremes broke through with a string of record hits, they got offers to appear on TV, and in the big night clubs. Here, Motown stepped in, and hired professionals who helped them develop some more original dance-patterns that would give them more individuality and gloss as an "act." Today, of course, when Diana appears as a single on TV, or plays the big clubs and prestige hotels, she has the pick of top choreographers. They think up more original dance concepts. And Diana does a nice brisk job on routines that are far more complicated than "pop group choreography." Trade paper reviews of her act since she stepped out as a solo applaud her ability to move out on the floor.

Pam Migliore
Torrence, California

Q. *How many albums does Diana Ross have out now?*

A. The many albums Diana made with the Supremes are still selling on records and on cassettes. Since she started out on her own in 1970, Diana Ross has produced one album titled simply *Diana Ross*. There's a photograph of her as a little girl in Detroit on the LP jacket. She has also recorded a bestselling single "Ain't No Mountain High Enough." More Diana Ross records are coming.

POP STAR INVESTMENTS

Ann Kunicki
Forest Hills, New York

Q. *I hear pop stars invest their money in lots of different ways. What are some of the things they are involved with, financially?*

A. You name it, and they've got money in it. Frank Sinatra, probably the wealthiest single figure in pop, has money in radio and TV stations, motion pictures, real estate, music publishing, stocks. Herb Alpert bought the old Charlie Chaplin movie studio in Hollywood and turned it into A & M Records, of which he is coowner. James

Herb Alpert

Brown has money in food stores; he is board chairman of Gold Platter, Inc., and Penny Pantry, a 12-store Georgia food chain. Brown also owns at least one radio station. Joan Baez is a backer of the Institute for the Study of Non-Violence, Palo Alto, California. Eydie Gorme and Steve Lawrence have backed the building of resort motels in Puerto Rico.

A lot of Chuck Berry's money is tied up in an amusement area complex outside St. Louis, which has facilities for picnicking, dancing, swimming. Remember Roger Miller, the country singer-songwriter who journeyed to fame with his record, "King of the Road"? If you recall, that song told of the rough time you can have when you're on the road, and you don't have any money. Well, the singer, product of a broken home, has recently opened up a snazzy, palatial, million-dollar "King of the Road Motel Hotel" in Nashville. The carpets there are thicker than country molasses. And Burt Bacharach, the handsome, talented, composer-recording star is not exactly a weight-watcher. From money he has earned on such songs as "What the World Needs Now," "The Look of Love," and "Do You Know the Way to San Jose?" he has bought two restaurants. They are the Dover House (specializing in sea food) and Rothmann's, a vintage eating landmark — both on Long Island, New York. Sports appeals to Bobbie Gentry ("Ode To Billie Joe") as a field for investment. She has record-royalty money invested in the Phoenix Suns, a pro-basketball team in Arizona.

NANCY WILSON

Jackie Lopez
New York, New York

Q. *How did Nancy Wilson get started?*

A. Nancy Wilson was born February 20, 1937, in Chillicothe, Ohio, and started to sing almost as soon as she started to talk. "I've always sung; I just couldn't keep quiet. I sang anything anytime anybody would listen." She knew she wanted to be a singer from the age of four. She lived with her grandmother, and there was music everywhere around. Her aunts came to visit and played the piano and organ and said to the little Nancy, "Come on, sing." And Nancy did.

As a teenager Nancy sang in church choirs; she sang with her friends in quartets that they put together; she entered contests. She won a contest. That's when Nancy's public life began. As a result of winning the contest, she was given exposure on a local TV station in Columbus, Ohio. A passion to perform was born. From then on Nancy would have but one goal in mind — one aim that would drive her day and night until she achieved it — to be a star. Nancy was only fifteen, but the local clubs were bidding for her; she was beginning the long hard road to the success she now can call her own.

In April 1960, Capitol signed her to a long term recording contract. Since then she has produced more than 30 albums, singing the better quality pop tunes, jazz material, show tunes with taste and style. She's an example of the type of recording artist represented by Frank Sinatra, Andy Williams, Tony Bennett. They may not figure in the singles market too much, but they are steady consistent sellers among album buyers. Lately, she has branched out as a TV personality, exhibiting a flair for comedy. She delighted video fans with her put-ons and acting in comedy sketches, satirizing everything from soap operas to prejudice on the Carol Burnett CBS-TV program.

CHUCK BERRY

Mike Clyne
Oak Lawn, Illinois

Q. *Although I was too young to know about Chuck Berry's songs when they were recorded, I have since heard many of them and I like them very much. I particularly enjoy "School Days," which is still appropriate today. And now for the questions. Where was Chuck Berry born?*

A. The 6 foot 1 inch singer-writer-guitarist, Chuck Berry (Charles Edward Berry), was born in St. Louis, Missouri. His birthday is October 18. He came from a family steeped in music. His dad, Henry, a carpenter by trade, was bass singer in Antioch Baptist Church, St. Louis. His mother, Martha, was a soprano in the same choir. Chuck has three sisters: Lucy Ann who was a leading contralto and pianist; Thelma, another sister, also a pianist; and Martha, who sings with him occasionally on his records ("Come On," "Go, Go, Go"). His two brothers, Henry, Jr. and Paul L., also enjoyed singing. Chuck Berry credits his music teacher, Mrs. Julia Davis, with getting him jobs as a singer-guitarist. Chuck actually began singing as a bass with the Glee Club of Sumner High School in St. Louis.

Q. *Where does he live now?*

A. Chuck lives now in Chicago when not on the road. But he spends a good deal of his extra time managing his growing amusement center, Berry Park, at Wentzville, Missouri, 40 miles west of St.

Louis. It's a miniature Coney Island and caters
mostly to black people in and around St. Louis.
Berry first bought the acreage there more than
ten years ago. Since then he has purchased more
than 100 nearby acres to expand his holdings. Today, most of the land is cleared and is utilized in
the outdoor park and indoor clubhouse and night-
club operation. The park reportedly holds about
2,000 people. Berry can be seen around the park
trimming the grass, uprooting weeds, operating
the loud speaker system.

Berry records for Chess, which has specialized
in rhythm and blues since 1949, along with such
little known labels of the time as National, Savoy,
Atlantic, and King. Berry pioneered in moving

rhythm and blues into the world of teens. Thus he wrote and recorded "Johnny B. Goode," "Carol," "Almost Grown," "Rock and Roll Music," "Sweet Little Sixteen," and of course "School Days." If you're not familiar with his million selling 1957 "Golden Oldie," here's how it goes:

Up in the mornin' and out to school
The teacher is teachin' the Golden Rule
American History and practical math
You study 'em hard, hopin' to pass
Workin' your fingers right down to the bone
And the guy behind you won't leave you alone.

© 1957 Arc Music Corporation (BMI)

Q. *Is Chuck Berry married?*

A. Yes.

CHICAGO

Greg Romano
Watertown, Connecticut

Q. *How did you get your name?*

A. The band developed in Chicago under the name of the Big Thing. At the time, people in clubs and at dances were not receptive to the group's efforts. The act was nearing a dead end in the city of its origin. As its style began to change it became evident that it would have to leave. James William Guercio, the record producer, thought the sheer activity present within the Los Angeles music scene would benefit the group. Guercio brought them out West, changed the name to Chicago Transit Authority, moved them into a small house in Hollywood, telling them to worry only about their music and nothing else. However, now they're just called Chicago.

HOW TO GET SONGS RECORDED

Bonnie Darst
Amanda, Ohio

Q. *I've been thinking of letting you [Bobby Sherman] look over my song I wrote specially for you. You could tell me what you think of it and then, someday, when my friend and I get going we'll write some of your songs for you; that is, if you like the first one. I once wrote a song in one day. But only my friends read it. They thought I really had what it took. I'm worried about people claiming songs that aren't really protected by some laws or patents, or something.*

A. Many young amateur songwriters wrote asking the same question of other artists. They asked how to sell original songs. Some even enclosed song lyrics. Generally, pop stars or groups will not look at unsolicited, unasked for songs on music manuscript, or handwritten, or typed song lyrics mailed to them. The pop song stars, along with their disc producers, want to hear what the song sounds like on record.

As to copyrighting, here's the situation. Song titles cannot be copyrighted. Countless numbers of people can write songs with the same title without being in trouble legally. But music and lyrics can be copyrighted either together or singly. However, many of today's pro songwriters do not copyright material until a record is secured. Others argue that today's pop people are more likely to look at copyrighted material from unknown writers, so it's worth the effort and expense.

That's the state of song selling today. So what can you do? The best thing is to put your song on a demonstration record. Record producers, many of whom can't read music, and pop stars prefer to listen to new material on these "demos." Send your record to: (1) key record companies; attention A & R Department (2) specific record producers. You can find the names and the addresses in the feature, "Vital Statistic," published weekly by *Cash Box*. Look for the word PROD. in the list of top-selling records. (3) Music publishers.

Keep in mind that song writing is a brutally competitive business. Shrewd music publishers and songwriters use all kinds of angles to have their new songs used by the top groups. They romance the top singers and talk up their material. The top groups like to sing material by known hit writers. Also, many of the pop groups write their own material. So the chances of an outsider making it are just that, an outside chance. The truth is that selling songs is an art in itself. It takes time, patience, contacts, and luck. Most professional songwriters live in and around the centers of record production: New York, Detroit, Nashville, Los Angeles. Trying to sell songs by mail is as difficult as using rubber cement for a concrete patio. You've got to be where the action is — meet the record producers, talk to fellow songwriters, get to learn song writing as a business. But, if you feel strongly about writing songs, try to learn as much as possible. Song writing is a craft which requires constant study. Take music courses, learn to play an instrument, study composition, study the Top Ten hits, hear what is selling, analyze the better songs carefully both for music and lyrics. Don't be afraid of originality. If you are ever in the position of having somebody interested in your work professionally, there is the matter of getting a good music publishing contract that protects you. The best songwriter contracts are those prepared by the American Guild of Authors and Composers (AGAC), 50 West 57th Street, New York, N.Y. 10019. It's run by songwriters. Richard Rodgers, Alan Jay Lerner, Duke Ellington, Johnny Cash, and Bob Dylan belong to it.

Later on, if you ever get songs recorded, you will hear about two organizations — The American Society of Composers, Authors, and Publishers (ASCAP), and Broadcast Music, Inc. (BMI). They are organizations to which songwriters belong. They collect royalties for the songwriters and publishers from radio, TV, restaurants, resorts, from anyplace, in fact, that uses music for profit. The songwriter will get paid from these music licensing pools depending on how popular his material is and how often it is used on radio and TV. Songwriters also get credit from ASCAP and BMI for songs which reach the Top Ten.

THE FRIJID PINK

David Steinberg
Philadelphia, Pennsylvania

Q. *What do you think about music lessons? Are they important for pop music?*

Gary R. Thompson, lead guitar: I don't think music lessons are important because they leave out the ability to create your own style. Whoever you learn from, you automatically pick up his style of playing. Rock music is the ability to play in a free manner, not to be tied down to notes on a piece of paper.

Kelly Green, vocals: I really don't think music lessons are that important in pop music, unless you are going to major in music later in life at college or something. But I do recommend though, a few music lessons, just to get the major chords and notes. So at least you won't be a half-baked musician in writing and arranging.

Satch Harris, bass guitar: Music lessons are good

for the average, run of the mill person, I guess, but I feel if you have the talent you don't need them, except in the beginning. Most of the time you get sick of someone trying to teach you "Mary Had a Little Lamb" and junk like that. I must admit, though, they help when we are trying to write out lead sheets for our music.

Rick Stevens, drums: As far as music lessons for pop music goes, the people who are playing pop music now have not necessarily had music lessons, but have had music lessons in school for concert music, depending on the instrument, and sometimes this helps considerably. As far as guitar goes, most people who I know haven't had lessons, but have been playing for a long time and know a lot about the instrument and music from teaching themselves. Lessons really come in handy when you learn the fundamentals in music and this can help you to find your own style in writing and arranging. I might add that lessons are only good if the person teaching music knows how to teach. If lessons have been decided upon they should be started at an early age. The earlier the better.

Q. *How did you get started?*

Gary: I myself started playing drums and finally got tired of banging around, and wanted to play something to produce music. I started playing guitar because all my friends did. We sort of taught each other things we would pick up. But not giving lessons to each other. It was more like "Hey, guess what, pal? I found out that if you pull a G string on the 9th position you can get a weird sound." And that's where it started.

Kelly: Well, I've been singing ever since I've started school. But about 11 years ago I started a local group playing drums and singing. After that group broke up about six weeks later, I met brother Gary and we've been together ever since. We did all the local dances around town, jumping from group to group, him playing guitar and me singing. I got off the drums 'cause I could put more feeling into singing. Then about three years ago we met Rick and Satch and formed the Frijid Pink. And the rest is history. Ha ha.

Satch: I got started about seven years ago, playing guitar for some local groups in Michigan. I played rhythm guitar for about two or three years. Two friends came up to me at the local hang-out and asked me to play bass for them. Time passed and so did the groups, and then came Frijid Pink and that's where I'm at now.

Rick: I got started back in school in third grade, a few years back and have had both school lessons and private, but only for concert, not rock and roll. I got my start in rock music when I went down to a basement one day and heard a group playing and said to myself . . . "that's what I want to do." By the time I got enough money together to buy some drums I was fifteen and I've been at it ever since.

Q. Do you work every day at your music?

Gary: I not only work every day, but every minute I possibly can. If you have to be forced to play you might as well hang it up. Music is an art. You have to love and believe in what you're doing. You'll know when you love it, because you can't do without it.

Kelly: I not only work at music every day, I live it, breathe it, eat it, and sleep it. Why? Because music is my life. I love it or wouldn't be in it if I didn't.

Satch: I practice every chance I get and then sometimes that's not enough. I try to get in at least four or five hours a day every day. It's very hard to do because of our very tight schedule.

Rick: One way or another, on the road travelling it's hard to practice drums, so I bought a guitar and mess around with it when I have the chance. However, if we pull into a city early enough I usually practice on drums some, time permitting. I don't sing much in the group, but I enjoy it and sing to just about everything on the radio, if you call that working on your music. Hotels seem to frown on jamming in your rooms for some reason or other. Ha ha.

Q. *How do you feel when performing before an audience?*

Gary: It's the greatest feeling in the world and the hardest to explain. You feel good because you're pleasing someone else and yourself at the same time. You also feel honored that the audience is there to hear you in the first place, so you want to do your best. It's really hard to say. I guess you sorta feel like an idol or something.

Kelly: It is really a nice feeling to get up on stage and play in front of an audience and know that they're digging your music. Because music is communication, and if you see the people like your music, you feel great because you know you've put something across. It's just a beautiful feeling.

Rick: I think it's the greatest thing there is in the world. It really makes me feel super when you can feel the music on your body. Music seems like a hot line to your head that says "Don't just sit there, dummy, move!" It seems like you have hundreds of people in your group all at one time on stage, dancing, singing, and doing whatever the hell they want.

Satch: I can only say I feel great, fantastic, right on, and whatever else you can say that goes along with playing for people who appreciate and get into it with you. I feel the best when people come up on stage with us until it's overflowing and the rest of the audience is standing and screaming for more. In my mind I know that the group has done its best to please someone else, and that's where it's at, if you have given someone pleasure and happiness even if it's only for a moment.

136

NANCY SINATRA

Anthony Matiango
Springfield, Massachusetts

Q. *How did Nancy Sinatra get into show business?*
A. Being the daughter of Frank Sinatra helped. From the time she was a little girl, she has lived in a show business atmosphere of songs, night clubs, movies, TV specials, radio. Words like "openings," "an act," "contracts," "agents," "material" came with her toddler toys and dolls. When she was a little girl, in fact, a hit song was written about her, "Nancy with the Laughing Face." It was originally written for her birthday — a vocal touch for a private family affair. But later, during World War II, it became a hit. The Sinatra name, of course, opened many doors and gave her many opportunities. But to her credit, this 5'3", small-boned daughter of a legend studied dancing, singing, acting, and worked hard to make it on her own. Of course, once you get the opportunity you must please an audience — record buyers, TV audiences. And here the Sinatra "name" cannot help. She has been married to Tommy Sands, one-time pop idol, now a favorite in Hawaii. She's been in a few films with no noticeable success. Her biggest triumphs have been on records. Her biggest record smash so far has been "These Boots Are Made for Walkin'."

There is a 95-minute documentary film made of that tour.

During this same period, too, Mick Jagger, the leader of the Stones was busy as an actor in motion pictures: *Performance, Sympathy for the Devil,* and one about Ned Kelly, leader of a gang of outlaws — all brothers.

You haven't been able to buy new Rolling Stones records for a while because of a bitter business dispute. The Stones have not been happy with Alan Klein, a New York pop entrepreneur who has had a contractual say in their recording contracts. The rock underground says that The Stones have desired a change in their record affiliation. They want to go from London to Atlantic or Chess — or perhaps develop their own label. Anyway, in the fall of 1970, just as the autumn breezes started, their fans were happy to greet a new album titled, *Get Yer Ya-Ya's Out.*

141

WHITE HOUSE POP

David Fiedler
Forest Hills, New York

Q. *How much do pop stars and groups make when they play the White House?*

A. No money at all. Singers and groups who put on shows on the White House stage do it for prestige. The White House does not even pick up hotel bills or travel expenses. So it costs pop groups money to entertain at a state occasion or a Presidential "evening of entertainment." But they get a lot of publicity. The White House staff has a thick file of entertainers in the world of pop, theatre, films, ballet, classical music; from Lincoln Center to Grand Ole Opry. The President himself chooses who is to appear at these gala evenings.

Some entertainers who have appeared at the White House include The Turtles, Carol Channing, Pearl Bailey, and Johnny Cash. (A request by President Richard Nixon that Cash sing "Welfare Cadillac," which poked fun at people on welfare, provoked a storm of protest.)

Generally, pop protest singers like Pete Seeger or groups are not welcome. However, an antiwar song from the Broadway musical hit, *1776,* was allowed at a special White House performance. There was some talk that President Nixon's White House staff would try to delete the song, "Momma Look Sharp," but it was not cut from the production when it was performed in the East Room.

THE BEATLES

Mark Houle
Springfield, Massachusetts

Q. *When will the next live performance of the Beatles be, and where?*

A. The future course of the Beatles is as unpredictable as a second-hand car. A few years ago, the famed quartet set up Apple Records at 3 Saville Road, London W. 1, England. It was supposed to be the seed of a vast Beatle entertainment-cultural complex. Hard-earned royalties were poured out, backing people and fun projects from records to boutiques. Waves of the now people rolled in: the pop people, the Carnaby Street crowd, promoters with schemes, and new artists with new songs. However, the Beatle magic did not automatically transfer to other projects and other people. Vast sums were lost. Today Apple is down to a core. It is as quiet as an unused recording studio. Few people work there. Letters go unanswered. The Beatles' press agent, for instance, went away to write his memoirs. According to the London *Daily Express,* "A lot of the staff has resigned out of sheer boredom."

Some say the Beatles will never be together again, that they are finished as a performing pop group. Each of them is pursuing a solo path as a record artist and as an actor. Sid Bernstein, the concert promoter who produced the historic Beatles concerts at Shea Stadium in New York, says: "My hunch is that they'll never perform together again."

About the future, Ringo Starr says one thing one day, and another, the next day. He told one reporter: "We are as united as we ever were, and nobody wants a split. The general public doesn't want us to split. And the Beatles don't want one, really, either." The next day he will say, "If you ask me, I'd say there is no group called the Beatles." In September 1970, Paul himself wrote a letter to London's *Melody Maker,* and said flatly, "Will the Beatles get together again? . . . No."

If the Beatles do not perform or record together as a pop group anymore, however, there is much unreleased material on tape. Stu Ginsburg of Capitol Records, which distributes the Beatles discs, says, "I've been told that there are 30 unmixed songs in Apple Studios."

Q. *Why did Paul go away from the group?*
Paul: The party is over — but no one really wants to announce its finish. I didn't leave the Beatles — the Beatles left the Beatles. First Ringo left during our recording of the "white album" because he said that it wasn't fun anymore. Then George left because he thought that we were not saying enough on *Abbey Road.* John fell in love with Yoko and out of love with the rest of us.

(Paul McCartney reportedly did not like the influence of Yoko, John's new Japanese wife, over the Beatles. He also did not care for Allen Klein, the Beatles' new manager, who succeeded the late Brian Epstein. McCartney proposed that the British group be handled by his father-in-law, a prominent, canny New York City theatrical attorney and music publisher, Lee Eastman. Paul is married to Linda Eastman. But the other Beatles batted that suggestion down.)

G. Slotnick
Wantagh, New York

Q. *How old are each of the Beatles?*
A. Here are the facts on the creators of Beatlemania:

John Lennon — He's 30. John Ono Lennon was born on October 9, 1940, in Oxford Street Maternity Hospital, Liverpool, England. He plays guitar, organ, piano, and harmonica. He has brown hair and brown eyes and is 5'11".

Paul McCartney — James Paul McCartney is 28. He was born on June 18, 1942, in Liverpool. He has one brother, Michael. He plays guitar,

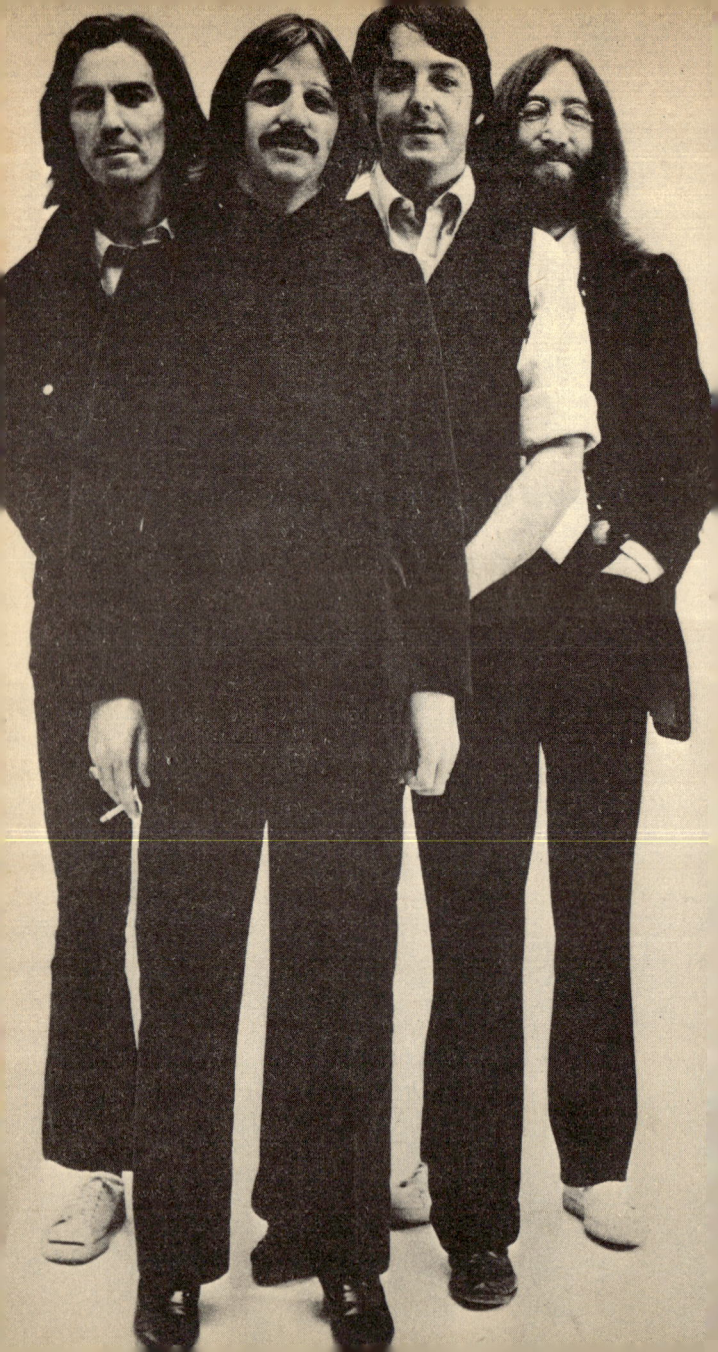

piano and organ. He has very dark brown hair and brown eyes and is 5'11".

George Harrison — George Harrison is 30. He was born on February 25, 1943 at 12 Arnold Grove, Wavertree, Liverpool, England. He has two brothers, Harold and Peter, and one sister, Louise. He plays guitar, organ, and a variety of Indian instruments. He has brown hair and brown eyes and is 5'11".

Ringo Starr — Richard Starkey is 30. He was born on July 7, 1940 at 9 Madryn Street, Dingle, Liverpool, England. He is the group's percussionist. He has brown hair and blue eyes and is 5'8".

Melanie Taborisky
Commack, New York

Q. *What do the Beatles think about marriage?*

A. Apparently they are for it very much. John Lennon has been married twice. His latest wife is the Japanese artist, Yoko Ono. He married her in Gibraltar, on March 20, 1969. Paul McCartney is married to Linda Eastman, a pretty, blonde, ex-fan magazine photographer. The McCartney's have two daughters: one from Linda's previous marriage, and Mary, the first child of their own. They were married at the Marylebone Register Office on March 12, 1969. George Harrison is no bachelor, either. He married Patricia Anne Boyd at the Epsom Register Office, Surrey, on January 21, 1966. Ringo Starr is a family man, too. He and his wife Maureen have two sons: Zak, 4, and Jason, 2. They are expecting a third child. The Ringo Starrs live in luxury. He owns three homes and, for his latest birthday, his wife got him a remote country cottage. They were married at Caxton Hall, London, on February 11, 1965.

Les Copley
Myrtle, West Virginia

Q. *How did the Beatles get started?*

A. The drab factory town of Liverpool produced pop's biggest glamour group, the Beatles. John, Paul, and George were schoolboy friends with an interest in the pop idols of the period — Elvis Presley, Chuck Berry, and Bill Haley. Together they went to the Liverpool rock clubs where the big beat was becoming as big as fish'n'chips. In the late '50's, John and Paul decided to form a two-man group called the Nurks (slang for low-life in the RAF). Later on George joined up and the trio became known as the Quarrymen. They got jobs in and around Liverpool for very little money. In 1958, they added a good-looking drummer, Pete Best, who attracted the "birds." When Best got sick, a young drummer, named Ringo Starr, subbed.

At varying times, the group changed its name from the Quarrymen to the Skiffle Group, Johnny and the Moondogs, and the Moonshiners. In 1960, a job offer came through to play Hamburg, Germany, for $15 a week per man. By then the quartet was a five-man group with a bass guitar player, Stuart Sutcliffe. There, they created a splash in a Hamburg dive, the Kaiserkeller. It was during an engagement in Germany that Sutcliffe dreamed up the new name, Beatles — patterned after the other "animal" groups like Buddy Holly and the

Crickets. Soon after Stuart dropped out. He died of a brain hemorrhage at 22.

While in Germany, they cut their first recordings as a backup band for a pop singer, Tony Sheridan. One of these tunes was "My Bonnie." In October 1961 a customer walked into a record department of a Liverpool furniture store run by Brian Epstein and asked for the disc. Epstein didn't have it. Later he discovered that it was recorded by an English group in Germany called the Beatles. Shortly thereafter he went to a club — the Cavern — not far from his family's furniture store, to hear the group. The official press biography of the Beatles states that Epstein "discovered" the madcap group in Germany, at the Indra Club. Whichever version is right, Epstein took over personal management of the youthful Liverpudlians. In 1962, the group was finally locked into shape when Pete Best was replaced by Ringo Starr. A frustrated actor with good contacts among England's music tradepapers, Epstein poured his energy into the Beatles. He talked them up and finally got them a contract with E.M.I., perhaps the world's largest recording company, and also major stockholder of the U.S. label, Capitol. Soon the Beatles boom was underway.

Their first recording for E.M.I., "Love Me Do," was issued on the company's Parlaphon label in October 1962. It sold a respectable 100,000 copies. It was the last time a Beatle single sold less than a half-million. Their first (English) million-seller, "She Loves You," came out in the spring of 1963. It was followed by two albums, *Please, Please Me* and *With the Beatles*. Both LP's sold over 300,000 copies. Then, finally, came the unprecedented success of their recording of "I Want To Hold Your Hand," the first U.S. single (and the first million-seller in the U.S.). Since that time, it has been one million-seller after another.

Tom Van Diem, Jr.
Lansing, Michigan

Q. *How many Gold Records do the Beatles have?*
A. The million seller list compiled by the Record Industry Association of America reports that the Beatles have won Gold Records for the following singles and LP's:

1964   *Meet the Beatles*
       "I Want To Hold Your Hand" (S)
       "Can't Buy Me Love" (S)
       The Beatles Second Album
       Something New

"A Hard Day's Night" (S)
"I Feel Fine" (S)
Beatles '65
The Beatle's Story
1965 *Beatles VI*
Help
"Help" (S)
"Eight Days A Week" (S)
"Yesterday" (S)
Rubber Soul
1966 "We Can Work It Out" (S)
"Nowhere Man" (S)
Yesterday and Today
"Paperback Writer" (S)
Revolver
"Yellow Submarine" (S)
1967 "Penny Lane" (S)
Sergeant Pepper's Lonelyhearts Band
Magical Mystery Tour
"Hello Goodbye" (S)
1968 "Hey Jude" (S)
The Beatles
1969 *Yellow Submarine*
"Get Back" (S) with Billy Preston
Abbey Road
"Something" (S)
"Ballad of John and Yoko" (S)
1970 *Hey Jude*
"Let It Be" (S)
McCartney
Let It Be
36 Total Gold Records
18 singles
18 albums

ELVIS PRESLEY

G. Slotnick
Wantagh, New York

Q. *What is Elvis' real name?*

A. Elvis Presley is not a stage name. Actually, the tall, rangy, six-foot, hazel-eyed singer-actor is the surviving member of a set of twins. His full name is Elvis Aron Presley. He was born on January 8, 1935, which makes the King of Rock 'n' Roll 35 years old now. His parents are Gladys and Vernon Presley.

Q. *Is he self-taught?*

A. Yes. He started picking out on his guitar tunes that he heard over the radio, or on records. He has no formal musical training.

Patricia Erickson
Shady Valley, Tennessee

Q. *How did Elvis get started acting and singing?*

A. As a young boy in Tupelo, Mississippi, Presley often sang in church. He later joined his mother and father in a family trio singing religious songs. The Presleys sang at camp meetings, revivals, and church conventions. When the boy won a music contest at a local country fair by singing "Old Shep," his parents bought him his first guitar. It cost $12.98.

In 1953, Elvis, then a high school graduate, got a job as a $35 a week truck driver for the Crown Electric Company in Memphis. That year the 18-year-old, tall, well-built youth wandered into the Sun Recording Company to make a solo recording for his own private use. One year later, he was asked to make a record for Sun as a professional. On the basis of that record, called "That's Alright Mamma," he was taken under the shrewd direction of Colonel Tom Parker, who has remained his manager to this day. In the fall of 1955, RCA bid for the young performer's contract and got it for $35,000, a then unheard of price for a virtually untried artist.

This turned out to be one of the biggest bargains in show business. In 1958, Uncle Sam called Elvis to the army. It was predicted that Elvis' absence would be his downfall. The columnists and the mass media speculated that the fans would forget him. However, the Elvis bubble didn't burst. His two year stint in Europe was extensively covered by magazines and newspapers. Also, before he went away, RCA cannily got Elvis

to cut quite a few records. And so, the turntables were hotly spinning new Presley products while he was in khaki. Furthermore, Elvis won grudging admiration from respectable middle-America because he didn't go into special services as an entertainer, but served as an ordinary G.I. in a truck detachment.

Elvis Presley, the country boy who packaged country music with black rhythm and blues, has become one of the top record sellers of all time. He has sold more than Enrico Caruso, Glenn Miller, and Toscanini put together. The RCA catalogue lists 48 gold records (each representing more than a millon records sold worldwide) for Elvis. More than 250,000,000 copies of Elvis Presley recordings have been sold all over the world in the 15 years he has recorded exclusively for RCA. Thirty-two motion pictures starring Elvis Presley have been released to date. The highest fee ever paid for a single guest appearance on television, $125,000, went to Elvis in 1960 on the *Frank Sinatra Show*. In addition to his single gold records, Elvis has had ten albums certified as Gold Records by the Record Industry Association of America. One LP, *Blue Hawaii* is approaching the 3,000,000 sales mark.

Q. *What are Elvis' hobbies?*

A. Elvis lives a guarded, private life. He refuses to be interviewed. Even biographers of Presley can't get to see him. He reportedly has never become part of the Hollywood scene. He is married to the daughter of an Air Force colonel, Priscilla Beaulieu. They have a three-year-old girl, Lisa Marie. Some say that Elvis makes $5,000,000 a year, some say he earns double that. He likes to be alone with friends from the South. The group that surrounds him has been called "The Memphis Mafia." He has a big home in California, and an enormous mansion called Graceland just outside of Memphis. The house is painted a kind of phosphorescent blue and gold that glows at night. Elvis loves cars. At different times he's owned motorcycles, a gold Cadillac, a Rolls Royce, and a luxurious trailer bus. He has donated a great deal of the Presley royalties to charities, most of which operate in his own hometown of Memphis; it is done without much publicity, but there has never been a break in either his interest or participation in these organizations' activities.

Q. *What does Elvis think of the generation gap?*

A. Bob Hope, Pete Seeger, John Wayne, Joan Baez, Tommy Smothers — all comment on politics and public affairs. But not Elvis. On the race issue, the Viet Nam war, choices for president, he has remained silent. He is not a political person, and if he has a point of view he does not make it public. As an entertainer and record star, of course, Elvis has reached across the generations. He continues to be popular with fans of different ages who go to see his movies and buy his records.

BROOK BENTON

Janet Felicia Carloss
Wisner, Louisiana

Q. *I chose to write to you about Brook Benton because I love to hear him sing, "Don't It Make You Wanna Go Home?" How long has Brook been singing?*

A. Brook is a veteran pop singer and songwriter.

Most know him because of his recent smash, "Rainy Night in Georgia." But he has been hitting the Top Ten charts for more than a decade. In 1959, he recorded a ballad, "It's Just a Matter of Time," which reached the charts. Following this, he got into a fabulous golden groove with a succession of 12 hits within two years. During that period, he was the top male black singer of the record business, along with Jackie Wilson and Harry Belafonte. Then things got a little slow for Brook. The young rock groups took over almost completely, particularly in the singles market. But in 1970 Brook burst forth again with "A Rainy Night in Georgia." The disc was cut in Miami — a new pop recording center made popular by Atlantic-Cotillion Records.

Q. *What does he do in his spare time? What other type of job does he have besides singing?*

A. Brook makes a living singing, recording, and writing songs. In his spare time, he helps young people. He has been active in Rochdale Village, an interracial housing project in a heavily black neighborhood in St. Albans, Long Island, New York. Anxious to do something positive, he conceived of a talent hunt among young people who were just hanging around. He helped with advice, contacts, direction, tips. Some of his protégés have gotten jobs off-Broadway. He also helped establish the St. Albans Choir, a vocal group of 40 young people between the ages of 11–14. Brook even recorded a Christmas song with the choir. He is married and a member of the American Guild of Authors and Composers. He writes many of his songs while in bed.

SIMON AND GARFUNKEL

Diana "Albert" Thomas
Syracuse, New York

Q. *I read an unfavorable review of your album*
Bridge Over Troubled Waters. *I know that re-*
views sometimes are mean, but are they supposed
to be cruel? I wish that he (or any other critic who
didn't like a song or an album) wouldn't rip it
apart for people who enjoy it.

Art: You can write a dissertation on this. Everybody is entitled to his own opinion. A reviewer
writes what he feels like writing. That's his job.

Q. *How did Art Garfunkel tape the voices of old*
people on the Bookends *album? Did he do it*
alone or did Paul Simon help? Also, did he just
talk to people and have the recorder right there?

Paul: The album *Bookends* was done several years ago and released in 1968. Artie took a tape recorder to homes for the aged. He went to the United Home for Aged Hebrews and the California Home for the Aged at Reseda. I also went with him to Central Park in New York, with the tape recorder, taping the voices and thoughts of old people. In all of these places Art interviewed people about old age.

David Seidman
Takoma Park, Maryland

Q. *How did Simon and Garfunkel get together?*

A. They met in the sixth grade at P.S. 164 in Forest Hills, Queens, New York. It's a middle-class suburb. Later they gave concerts before more than 20,000 people at the Forest Hills Tennis Stadium, not far from where they used to go to elementary school. They got to know each other while acting in that unpaid, but lively, form of show business — a school play. The school had whipped up a graduation spectacular, *Alice in Wonderland*. Paul Simon played the White Rabbit, while Arthur (Art) cavorted around as the grinning Cheshire Cat. They also went to Hebrew school after classes, until they were Bar Mitzvahed. While at Hebrew school, Art began singing in the synagogue choir.

As both grew up they turned to rock and roll. They became followers of rock during the days of the late Alan Freed, a pioneering New York disc jockey who put on those rock dance programs on TV, and rock shows in theatres. "Neither of us," says Art, "was a group-type, except maybe in athletics. I guess that's why we were drawn together. We were going to rock 'n' roll shows when the audiences were mostly made up of kids from Harlem."

Later on, they grew closer together when both attended Forest Hills High School. Right after the music period they would blend voice and guitar; Paul would bring his guitar and Art would join in on the vocals. Paul started to write. And as a young teen twosome they had a modest hit with "Hey Schoolgirl," a kind of bubblegum rock song. They called themselves Tom and Jerry. Later, defying an old show business tradition, they changed their names back to their own — Paul Simon and Art Garfunkel. The rest is pop music history.

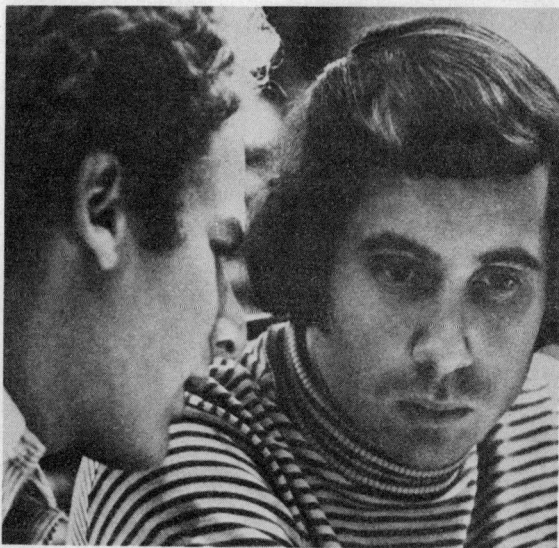

SAMMY DAVIS, JR.

Steven Rappleya
Springfield, Massachusetts
Q. *How did Sammy Davis get in show business?*
A. Sammy Davis came from a show business family. His father was a vaudeville dancer and his mother, Elvera Sanchez, a chorus girl. His mother left him when he was a little boy. He was born in Harlem on December 8, 1925. As a youngster he

watched the top black comedians of the day—Butterbeans and Susie; the Eight Black Dots; Pot, Pan and Skillet. He got to know the talented singers and dancers who graced all-black musical revues such as *Connie's Hot Chocolates* and *McKinney's Cotton Pickers*. Besides watching from the wings, he got to know firsthand the harsh conditions of black vaudeville—poor rooming houses, run-down hotels, tattered rooms with peeling paint that passed for dressing rooms. Yet, despite the conditions, there was much that was marvelous for any youngster slated to be in show business. For he was seeing the best black comedians, the black dancers, the black singers. While most of the kids were memorizing grammatical structures of verbs, he was memorizing songs, monologues, and punch lines.

Before he knew it he was on stage and dancing on black pumps with iron tap-tips. He danced and sang with his uncle, Will Mastin, in legitimate theatres, burlesque theatres, and carnivals. To confuse the truant officers who haunted theatres to watch for youngsters who should have been in school, he was sometimes called Silent Sam, the Dancing Midget. When he was seven years old, he had been in show business for four years.

Sammy, of course, has been active in all forms of entertainment—records, theatre, nightclubs, films, concerts, TV. In 1965 he published a book, *Yes I Can*. It's a classic American show business autobiography. In it Davis told a hidden story—how big name black entertainers were discriminated against by hotels and restaurants even as their names were up in lights in that same city.

ERIC CLAPTON

Su Wozniak
Danville, Illinois

Q. *Could you please tell me what Eric Clapton's future plans are? I'm 15, and truly a dedicated hard and heavy rock fan! I really admire Clapton, but it's quite difficult to follow him these days. Could you please tell me if he plans to go out on his own, join a group, start his own or what? I'd also appreciate knowing a little of his life history.*

A. His press biography says that "Eric Clapton never played a wrong note in the 25 years of his life." This could be a pure press puff, but there's no doubt that he's one of the best rock guitarists in the business. He was born in England, the son of a Surrey bricklayer. As a young man he attended art school, but he never was serious about art as a profession. Then he discovered the guitar — and it and rock bands became his life. In his early days he played with a number of unsuccessful rock bands, including a two-year stint as lead guitarist with Casey Jones and The Engineers. The blues-influenced guitarist became noticed as a member of the Yardbirds. When the Yardbirds drifted away from the blues, Clapton paid his rent by working as a studio musician.

Though he hated the superego trips of rock groups, he joined up as lead guitarist with another sideman he met — John Mayall. In 1966, while with Mayall, rock fans wrote on a London wall, "Clapton is God." However, the 5 foot 11 inch guitarist continued to be restless. He wanted to try a new mix of rock and the blues. So he formed the Cream (Ginger Baker and Jack Bruce), which reportedly sold more than 10 million records before it broke up. Later, Clapton hopscotched around with Blind Faith; The Plastic Ono Band; Delaney, Bonnie and Friends.

The B.B.C., which seldom goes overboard on anything, has called him "The most venerated musician in popular music." *Down Beat,* now the jazz-rock journal, equally impressed, recently said "Rarely has a rock instrumentalist working as a sideman made more of an impression on fellow musicians and audiences than Eric Clapton."

Typically his own view is: "I don't understand why anyone should claim anything for me. I am just a guitar player.

"Daily I hear things by other guitarists that really surprise me. And in the United States there

165

are dozens of guys down in the South that have pure genius. I have my own heroes, and I try to think when I am playing 'How would so and so have done this?' It's ridiculous to claim that I am the best guitarist in the world."

You ask what is he doing now? In the summer of 1970 Eric organized Derek and the Dominos, a four-piece rock group. Derek is, of course, Eric Clapton. Sometimes humorously nicknamed "Slowhand," because of the speed of his fingers on the guitar frets, he is hailed far and wide as the ultimate blues guitarist. But the cult hero of the guitar generation is desperately ducking and weaving to avoid being carried under by the sheer weight of his reputation.

The Dominos are not separate; each is equal with Derek. They are Bobby Whitlock, principally on organ, occasionally guitar, and all the time vocally supporting the lead singing of Eric Clapton; bassist Carl Radle; and drummer Jim Gordon, together one of the tightest rhythm sections around.

The links between the four were formed when Blind Faith toured America, with the yet-to-blossom Delaney, Bonnie and Friends. They were welded tight when that band came to Europe in last year's sensational trip with Eric, George Harrison, and Dave Mason, and they were finally sealed when Eric invited the Dominos over from England to play at the Dr. Benjamin Spock Civil Liberties Defense Fund concert. Since then they have been recording, rehearsing, and writing the material which will be the mainstay of their stage and club appearances.

BLOOD, SWEAT AND TEARS

Julie McMurtrie
Rothshild, Wisconsin
Q. *Where do you get your ideas for your cool songs? What is your favorite of all of them?*
Steve Katz: Some of our songs are written by our-

selves and some aren't. Those that aren't are chosen if they really knock all of us out. Then Dick Halligan or Fred Lipsius will arrange the song according to how they feel it. Changes in the arrangements and solo space are determined in rehearsal. I have no one favorite song.

Fred Lipsius: We have a repertoire meeting. Everybody brings in songs that they've heard on albums, or songs they've written themselves, or songs submitted by songwriters. Then the group votes on what they like. As to any particular favorite song, I have no favorites.

M. Strehlow
Ottawa, Kansas

Q. *What keeps a group together?*

Steve: Common denominators keep a group together. Mainly through hard work and our idea of good music do we share common goals. You also have to be friends with the people you work with.

Fred: The desire to create music and share it with others, and the fact that you can earn good money help keep a group together.

Q. *Why do people choose a profession as a rock recorder?*

Steve: I didn't actually choose it. I've loved music all my life and play a style of music that just happens to be commercial at the same time — because it's the popular music of my generation. I have been fortunate in being able to make a good living doing what I love most.

Fred: The many possibilities that the profession has to offer — creativity, fame, and fortune — plus more insight into the rock movement itself.

JOAN BAEZ

Susie Karlin
Kew Gardens, New York

Q. *Do you remember your first appearance before the public?*

Joan: I sang "Earth Angel" in the ninth grade assembly when I was 15 and I played it on the ukulele, and then for an encore I did "Honey Love," a slightly off-shade song. It was popular in those days. I was so nervous I never thought of it. I got up there. And all our mommies and daddies were out in the audience and there I was singing that dirty song!

Q. *What do you think of women's liberation?*
Joan: In spite of the fact that I have encountered so far the very least impressive, often repulsive side of women's lib, and in spite of the fact that *Time* magazine, as usual, took one half a sentence and placed it out of context, as is their fashion, I think that women's liberation is an obvious and urgent need. The difficulty for me is trying to make some sense out of the ends and means of an oppressed group of people, trying to gain insight into how a woman really becomes liberated in the context of this society. It is true I've been prone mostly to making wisecracks rather than becoming involved, but I feel this has been most short-sighted and am trying to re-examine my position.

Rita Rodriguez
Kansas City, Missouri
Q. *Did you always want to do your own thing? Or did you do as someone told you?*
Joan: I don't think it's possible to do your own thing when the rest of humanity is hungry, all shot up, and bleeding. No matter how hard you try not to, you still are involved.

Yvonne Taylor
Phoenix City, Alabama
Q. *How did you get started being a singer?*
Joan: The entertainment industry would have me tell you about "Joan Baez, the Folksinger," how I "got started," and where I've sung, and what laurels I have gathering dust under my bed.

But I'll tell you simply, that there is no "Joan Baez, the Folksinger."

There is me, 30 years old, my husband in prison for draft refusal and resistance organizing . . . me sitting here listening to Merle Haggard's "Sing Me Back Home" and thinking . . . about children dying in Viet Nam, Biafra, India, Peru, U.S.A. . . . about the wedding of the military and business worlds in America . . . a powerful unity which ravages, plunders, devastates, and swallows up human lives as necessary protein for its blind growth . . .

. . . about how narrow are the minds of men who want to claim the moon with an American flag the minute our boots touch ground . . . exclude . . . always exclude . . .

. . . and about the sad faces of the little seal pups who are drowning in the oil slick. . .

In the midst of all these things, how could I pretend to entertain you?

Sing to you, yes.

To prod you, to remind you, to bring you joy, or sadness, or anger. . . . And I will say . . . consider life. Give life priority over all other things. Over land. Over law. Over profit. Over promises. Over all things.

Q. *What kind of music do you like to listen to?*

Joan: Favorites change. Recently, I've been addicted to the music of a fellow named Van Morrison. He's been underground, until recently. And he's the closest thing to jazz I've ever liked, but he's far more. There's no way to describe him. He's his own guy. I really am crazy about Joe Cocker and I'll always be fond of Dylan's music, and a few others. The best songwriter? To me, Dylan always shines way far above anybody I've heard. And I think the Beatles do some nice stuff, like that song, "Let It Be!" It's beautiful

Q. *How do you like being a singer?*

Joan: To sing is to love and affirm, to fly and soar, to coast into the hearts of the people who listen, to tell them that life is to live, that love is there, that nothing is a promise, but that beauty exists, and must be hunted for and found.

RECORD PRICES

Robert Itkin
West Orange, New Jersey

Q. *What makes one record from a company cost more than another from the same company?*

Sol Handwerger, MGM Records: A lot depends on contractual requirements and obligations to the artist. Some artists get more royalty than others. Some may get five per cent of the retail price, some seven per cent, some higher. (The average artist royalties run roughly from five cents for singles to 25 cents per LP.) A Glen Campbell will have a higher royalty than an unknown artist. Also, one label of the same company may be a cheaper label with unknown or new artists. These records will cost less. Sometimes a particular record will be higher priced because it may cost a lot to make.

HOW TO REACH THE POP STARS

Larry Coe
Sequin, Texas

Q. *How can I write to the various pop stars I like? Such as Dean Martin, Dionne Warwick, The Temptations, Dave Clark 5, Chairman of the Board?*

A. Pop stars guard their privacy. They rarely if ever give out their home addresses. They mostly have unlisted telephone numbers. They all like fans, sell-out crowds at concerts, record buyers. But they naturally need a certain privacy to think, and quiet to work and relax. Therefore pop fans who want to know their home addresses are out of luck.

However, you can always write to the pop stars and groups in care of the record company for whom they record, or their business offices. The mail will be forwarded to them. For example:

Dean Martin: Warners-Reprise Records, 4000 Warner Blvd., Burbank, Calif.

Dionne Warwick: Scepter Records, 254 W. 54 Street, New York, N.Y.

The Temptations: Motown Records, 6290 Sunset Blvd., Los Angeles, Calif. 90028.

Dave Clark 5: Dave has quit the recording scene. Formerly head of one of Britain's top selling pop groups (35,000,000 discs), he now has turned actor, and is attending drama school in London. He may change his mind, but that is his current status:

Chairman of the Board: Invictus Records, 2601 Cadillac Tower, Detroit, Michigan.

Here are some other postal notes on who to contact where:

Alive and Kicking: Roulette, 17 W. 60th, New York, N.Y.

Alpert, Herb: A & M Records, 1416 N. La Brea, Hollywood, Calif. 90028

Americans, Jay and The: UA Records, 729 7th Ave., New York, N.Y.

Archies: RCA, 1133 6th Ave., New York, N.Y. 10036

Association: Warner Bros., 4000 Warner Blvd., Burbank, Calif.

Bacharach, Burt: A & M Records, 1416 N. La Brea, Hollywood, Calif. 90028

Badfinger: Apple Records, 3 Saville Rd., London W.1., England.

Beatles: Apple Records, 3 Saville Rd., London W.1., England.

Berry, Chuck: Chess Records, 320 E. 21st Street, Chicago, Ill. 60616

Blood, Sweat and Tears: Columbia Records, 51 W. 52nd Street, New York, N.Y. 10019

Blues Image: Atlantic Records, 1841 Broadway, New York, N.Y.

Bread: Elektra, 15 Columbus Circle, New York, N.Y.

Brown, James: King Records, 1540 Brewster Ave., Cincinnati, Ohio

Byrds: Columbia Records, 51 W. 52nd Street, New York, N.Y. 10019

Campbell, Glenn: Capitol Records, 1750 N. Vine Street, Los Angeles, Calif.

Cash, Johnny: Columbia Records, 51 W. 52nd Street, New York, N.Y. 10019

Cocker, Joe: A & M Records, 1416 North La Brea, Hollywood, California

Crosby, Stills and Nash: Atlantic Records, 1841 Broadway, New York, N.Y.

Doors, The: Elektra Records, 15 Columbus Circle, New York, N.Y.

Dylan, Bob: Columbia Records, 51 W. 52nd Street, New York, N.Y. 10019

Feliciano, Jose: RCA, 1133 6th Ave., New York, N.Y. 10036

Fifth Dimension: Bell Records, 1776 Broadway, New York, N.Y.

Friends of Distinction: RCA, 1133 6th Ave., New York, N.Y.

Gentry, Bobbie: Capitol Records, 1750 N. Vine Street, Hollywood, Calif.

Goldsboro, Bobby: UA Records, 729 7th Ave., New York, N.Y.

Grand Funk Railroad: Capitol Records, 1750 N. Vine Street, Hollywood, Calif.

Guthrie, Arlo: Warner Bros., 4000 Warner Blvd., Burbank, Calif.

Guess Who: RCA, 1133 6th Ave., New York, N.Y. 10036

Havens, Richie: MGM Records, 1350 Ave. of Americas, New York, N.Y. 10019

Humperdinck, Engelbert: London Records, 539 W. 25th St., New York, N.Y. 10001

Jackson 5: Motown Records, 6920 Sunset Blvd., Los Angeles, Cal. 90028

Jefferson Airplane: RCA, 1133 6th Ave., New York, N.Y. 10036

Jones, Tom: London Records, 539 W. 25th Street, New York, N.Y.

Led Zeppelin: Atco, 1841 Broadway, New York, N.Y. 10023

Lennon, John: Apple Records, 3 Saville Row, London W.1., England

McCartney, Paul: Apple Records, 3 Saville Row, London W.1., England

McKuen, Rod: Warners Records, 4000 Warner Blvd., Burbank, Calif.

Melanie: Buddah, 1650 Broadway, New York, N.Y. 10019

Moments: Stang Records, 106 W. Palisade Ave., Englewood, New Jersey

Osmond Bros: MGM Records, 1350 Ave. of Americas, New York, N.Y. 10019

Owens, Buck: Capitol, 1750 N. Vine Street, Hollywood, Calif.

Sandpipers: A & M Records, 1416 N. La Brea, Hollywood, Calif. 90028

Sherman, Bobby: Metromedia Records, 1700 Broadway, New York, N.Y.

Simon, Joe: Sound Stage Records, Hendersonville, Tenn.

Simon and Garfunkel: Columbia, 51 W. 52nd Street, New York, N.Y. 10019

Smith, O. C.: RCA, 6121 Sunset Blvd., Hollywood, Calif. 90028

Stevens, Ray: Barnaby Records, 51 W. 52nd Street, New York, N.Y. 10019

Supremes: Motown, 2648 W. Grand, Detroit, Michigan

Three Dog Night: Dunhill Records, 8255 Beverly Blvd., Los Angeles, Calif.

Turner, Ike and Tina: UA Records, 6920 Sunset Blvd., Hollywood, Calif. 90028

Who, The: Decca Records, 445 Park Ave., New York, N.Y.

Wonder, Stevie: Motown, 2457 Woodward Ave., Detroit, Michigan